P9-DCT-992

For current pricing information,
or to learn more about this or any Nextext title,
call us toll-free at **1-800-323-5435**
or visit our web site at www.nextext.com.

A CLASSIC RETELLING

The Adventures of
Huckleberry
Finn

by Mark Twain

Cover photograph: CORBIS/BETTMANN

Copyright © 2000 by Nextext®, an imprint of McDougal Littell, a Houghton Mifflin Company. All rights reserved.

No part of this work may be reproduced or transmitted in any form or by any means, electronic or mechanical, including photocopying and recording, or by any information storage or retrieval system without prior written permission of Nextext® unless such copying is expressly permitted by federal copyright law. With the exception of not-for-profit transcription in Braille, Nextext® is not authorized to grant permission for further uses of copyrighted selections reprinted in this text without the permission of their owners. Permission must be obtained from the individual copyright owners identified herein. Address inquiries to Manager, Rights and Permissions, McDougal Littell, P. O. Box 1667, Evanston, Illinois 60204.

Printed in the United States of America
ISBN 0-618-00374-6

3 4 5 6 7 8 9 — QKT — 05 04 03 02

Table of Contents

Civilizing Huck. — Miss Watson. — Tom Sawyer Waits.

Huck says that the Widow Douglas took him
in to teach him manners. He talks about his
feelings about the clothing, the supper, the
stories about Moses, and the spelling lessons
with Miss Watson, and then slips out the
window to meet his friend Tom.

*The Boys Escape Jim. — Tom Sawyer's Gang. —
Deep Plans.*

The boys run into Miss Watson's servant Jim
before they leave. They play a trick on him.
Then they meet their friends and form a band
of robbers.

do, they find the money Huck hid in the coffin.
In the uproar, Huck and Jim run away.

The King Went for Him. — A Royal Fight.

The king thinks Huck tried to lose the two
of them. Huck denies it. The duke and king argue
and accuse each other of hiding the money in
the coffin. When they're about to come to blows,
the king says he did it (even though he didn't—
Huck did).

Chapter 31

Another Plan. — News from Jim. — Old Memories.

They stop at a town called Pikesville. The king says
he'll check it out. In half a day, he says, the duke
and Huck can go ashore. When they do, Huck runs
back to the raft but cannot find Jim. A boy tells
him Jim was captured and sold to Silas Phelps. Huck
thinks about taking Jim back to Miss Watson. Then
he remembers his friendship and loyalty to Jim. Huck
feels it's more important to honor Jim's goodness
than to honor the law.

Still and Sundy-like. — Up a Stump. — A Problem.

When Huck reaches the Phelps home, the
mother comes running out. She thinks he is

someone else. Huck plays along. He learns
that they were expecting Tom Sawyer. He tells
them he's Tom and calls them Aunt Sally
and Uncle Silas.

Chapter 33

**A Slave Stealer. — Southern Hospitality. —
Tar and Feathers.**

Huck heads for town. He sees the real Tom Sawyer.
Tom is happy to learn that Huck never died. Huck
takes Tom's bags. Tom waits awhile before showing
up as a stranger. The real Tom says he's his own
brother, Sid Sawyer. The boys only hear about Jim
once. Jim had warned the family not to go to the
king and duke's play. Tom and Huck sneak out to
see what happened to the king and duke and
see them tarred and feathered.

Chapter 34

The Hut. — Outrageous. — Troubled with Witches.

Tom and Huck think of a plan to steal Jim.
They see a slave taking food to the hut where
Jim is chained. They ask the slave to show
them where Jim is, but they pretend not to know
Jim. They tell Jim that they plan to dig him
out at night.

because of Huck's note. Huck gets nervous and hot. Huck rushes out to warn Tom. They escape through the tunnel and run through the woods with the farmers after them. The farmers cannot see them in the dark. Huck and Tom hide in the bushes. They make it to their canoe, but Tom gets a gunshot wound in the leg, so Huck goes to get a doctor.

Chapter 41
The Doctor. — Uncle Silas. — Aunt Sally in Trouble.

When he wakes up, Huck goes to look for the doctor, but instead he runs into Uncle Silas. Huck says that he and "Sid" (Tom) were part of the chase. Silas takes Huck home rather than let him go find Tom. The farmers and their wives have all come to dinner to talk about the escape. Aunt Sally is worried about Tom. Huck has to stay in his room. He tries three times to leave, but each time returns to his room.

Chapter 42
Tom Sawyer Wounded. — The Doctor's Story. — Hand Out Them Letters.

Uncle Silas says that a letter came from Aunt Polly. Aunt Sally looks up and sees Tom, the doctor, and Jim coming up the road. Some men take Jim back to his cabin and lock him up. They tell Jim he will be sold. Meanwhile, Tom tells Aunt Sally the whole truth

*about their plan to help Jim escape. Just then
Aunt Polly walks in. She tells everyone who Tom
and Huck really are and says that Miss Watson
has died and freed Jim in her will.*

Chapter the Last

**Out of Slavery. — Paying the Captive. —
Yours Truly, Huck Finn.**

*Everyone makes a fuss over Jim and how he
helped the doctor heal Tom's leg. Tom gives him
forty dollars for his efforts and for being a
good prisoner. Huck thinks about his future. He
wonders about his father and learns that the
dead man they found on the houseboat early on
their trip was Huck's father, but Jim hadn't the
heart to tell him. Huck decides to leave soon
for a new adventure, because Aunt Sally wants
to adopt him.*

*Vocabulary words appear in boldface type and are
footnoted. Specialized or technical words and phrases
appear in lightface type and are footnoted.*

Background

The Mississippi River

The main waterway in the United States in the 1800s was the Mississippi River. The name, probably from Chippewa, means "large river." It runs 2,348 miles long, from upper Minnesota all the way down the middle of the country to Louisiana.

Ports along the river became important strongholds in frontier America in the days of the pioneers. People and supplies moved west along the rivers on flatboats and rafts, stopping at river ports along the way. In the 1830s, the time just before *The Adventures of Huckleberry Finn* was set, steamboats began moving up and down the river.

Mark Twain himself was born in a river town named Hannibal, Missouri. While in his twenties, Twain traveled down the Mississippi River on a steamboat to New Orleans, hoping to find adventure. Instead he ended up apprenticed to Horace Bixby, a pilot of a Mississippi riverboat.

Dialect of *Huckleberry Finn*

**"You don't know about me, without
you have read a book by the
name of 'The Adventures of Tom Sawyer,'
but that ain't no matter."**

**"Say—who is you? Whar is you?
Dog my cats ef I didn' hear sumf'n.
Well, I knows what I's gwyne
to do. I's gwyne to set down here
and listen tell I hears it agin."**

These are classic examples of Twain's use of dialect.

The term *dialect* refers to language the way it is spoken by a particular group or in a particular area of the country. Distinct spellings, pronunciations, and ungrammatical expressions are sometimes used by writers to give the feeling of a dialect.

Spellings	sumf'n (something)
	gwyne (going to)
	agin (again)
Pronunciations	I's
	didn'
	Whar
Ungrammatical	ain't no matter
Expressions	set down here
	I hears it agin

In the front of the novel, Twain placed a note to explain the way his characters talked. "In this book," he wrote, "a number of dialects are used, to wit: the Missouri Negro dialect; the extremest form of the backwoods South-Western dialect; the ordinary 'Pike-County' dialect; and four modified varieties of this last. The shadings have not been done in a hap-hazard fashion, or by guess-work; but painstakingly, and with the trustworthy guidance and support of personal familiarity with these several forms of speech." Without this note, Twain wrote, readers might think that all the characters "were trying to talk alike and not succeeding."

Characters and Settings

Mark Twain's story, like the river he writes about, floats from one place to another. The settings and characters glide smoothly into one another. Here is an overview of some of the main people and places included in *Huckleberry Finn*.

Pike's County Characters

Widow Douglas,
lady who took Huck in as a son.

Miss Watson,
a "tolerable slim old maid."

Judge Thatcher,
local judge who holds Huck's money.

Huck's Pap,
his father, who is a drunk and a scoundrel.

Main Characters

Huckleberry Finn,
friend of Tom Sawyer, living with Widow Douglas.

Jim,
Miss Watson's slave.

Tom Sawyer,
Huck's friend.

Slavery in America

The issue of slavery around the time *Huckleberry Finn* was written can be seen in what is called "the Dred Scott Decision." Dred Scott was a slave. His owner took him from Missouri, a slave state, into Illinois and Wisconsin, and then back to Missouri. Dred Scott sued his owner, claiming that by living in a "free" state (Illinois), he had become a free man.

The United States Supreme Court heard the case. Its decision was handed down on March 6, 1857, about 25 years before Mark Twain wrote *Huckleberry Finn.* Chief Justice Roger Taney ruled against Dred Scott, asserting that as a slave he had "no rights."

▲

Dred Scott His lawsuit dragged on for years and ignited controversy over slavery.

The decision was highly controversial. It widened the split in the country between the "free" northern states and the slave-holding southern states. In the novel, the hopes of Jim, Miss Watson's slave and Huck's friend, rise and fall depending on whether he is in Missouri (a slave state) or Illinois (a free state).

Mark Twain (1835-1910)

Born in 1835 as Samuel Langhorne Clemens, Mark Twain was four years old when his family moved to Hannibal, Missouri. (According to Twain, he based the character of Huck Finn on a boy he knew in Hannibal named Tom Blankenship.)

At age thirteen, after his father died, Clemens began to work in a local print shop. He began work on a riverboat at age twenty-three. He first traveled down the Mississippi River to New Orleans looking for adventure. When the Civil War erupted in 1861, it stopped most boat travel up and down the river, so Clemens went west, again looking for adventure.

Clemens started writing around this time and changed his name to "Mark Twain." The term

▲

The Author Engraving of Mark Twain.

"mark twain" comes from the language used on riverboats. It means that the water is deep enough for the boat to travel safely.

Twain soon began to make a name for himself by publishing stories. Then, in 1870, he married Olivia Langdon and began writing novels. *The Adventures of Tom Sawyer* was published in 1876, and *The Adventures of Huckleberry Finn* followed in 1884-85. These are considered his greatest works.

Mark Twain died on April 21, 1910.

Life of Mark Twain

1835—Samuel Langhorne Clemens is born in Florida, Missouri.

1839—His family moves to Hannibal, Missouri.

1857—Clemens travels the Mississippi River and learns to become a riverboat captain.

1863—He first uses the pen name "Mark Twain."

1870—Twain marries Olivia Langdon.

1876—*The Adventures of Tom Sawyer* is published.

1884–85—*The Adventures of Huckleberry Finn* is published.

1910—Twain dies in Connecticut.

The Adventures of
Huckleberry
Finn

Y̲ou don't know about me unless you have read a book called *The Adventures of Tom Sawyer.* That book was made by Mr. Mark Twain, and he told the truth, mainly. There was things he stretched, but mainly he told the truth. Now in the end of that book, Tom and me found the money that the robbers hid in the cave. It made us rich. We got six thousand dollars apiece—all gold. Well, Judge Thatcher, he took it and loaned it out at interest. It earned us each a dollar a day all year round.

Then the **Widow**[1] Douglas, she took me for her son. She wanted to make me more proper. It was rough living in the house all the time with all that properness. When I couldn't stand it any longer, I got into my old rags and left, *feeling free again.*

---

[1] **Widow**—woman whose husband has died and who has not remarried.

But Tom Sawyer[2] hunted for me. He said he was going to start a band of robbers. He said he would only let me join if I went back and lived with the widow. So I went back.

The widow cried over me, and called me a poor lost lamb. She called me a lot of other names, too, but she never meant no harm by it. She put me in them new clothes again, and I couldn't do nothing but sweat and feel all cramped up. Well, then, the old thing started up again. The widow rung a bell for supper, and you had to come on time. You had to wait for the widow to tuck her head and **grumble**[3] over the food, though there weren't really anything the matter with it.[4]

After supper she got out her book and learned me about **Moses and the Bulrushers.**[5] By and by she let out that Moses had been dead a long time, so then I didn't care no more about him.

Her sister, Miss Watson, a slim old maid, had just come to live with her. She sat me down with a spelling book. She worked me hard for an hour and I couldn't take it much longer. Miss Watson kept

---

[2] Tom Sawyer—Huck's friend; the two began their adventures in Twain's earlier book *The Adventures of Tom Sawyer*, published in 1876.

[3] **grumble**—mutter or complain in a low voice.

[4] The widow is saying prayers over the food, but Huck doesn't seem to understand that.

[5] **Moses and the Bulrushers**—the story of Moses as a baby, when the princess found him among the tall grass of the swamp.

telling me to sit up straight and don't put your feet up there and don't **scrunch**[6] up. Then she told me about the bad place, and I said I wished I was there. She got mad and said she would never say that. She was going to live so as to go to the good place. Well, I couldn't see no advantage in going where she was going, so I made up my mind I wouldn't try for it. I asked her if she thought Tom Sawyer would go to the good place. She said not by a long shot. I was glad about that, because I wanted him and me to be together.

I asked her if she thought Tom Sawyer would go to the good place. She said not by a long shot.

When I went up to bed, I tried to think of something cheerful. I put a candle by the window and sat down in a chair. The stars was shining and the leaves rustled. An owl, away off, who-whooed about somebody that was dead. It made the cold **shivers**[7] run over me. I got so scared, I wished I had company. Pretty soon a spider crawled up my shoulder. I flipped it off and it lit in the candle. Before I could save it, the fire burned it up. I didn't need anybody to tell me that that would **fetch**[8] me

---

[6] **scrunch**—to crouch or slump down.

[7] **shivers**—shaking as if from the cold.

[8] **fetch**—get.

some bad luck. I got up and turned around three times. Then I tied up a lock of my hair with a thread, to keep the witches away.

Well, after a long time I heard the clock away off in the town go boom—boom—boom—twelve licks. Pretty soon I heard a twig snap. I could just barely hear a *"me-yow! me-yow!"* So I called back, *"me-yow! me-yow!"* I put out the light and climbed out the window onto the shed. Then I slipped to the ground and crawled in among the trees. Sure enough, there was Tom Sawyer waiting for me.

CHAPTER TWO

We went tip-toeing along a path in the trees. When we passed by the kitchen, I fell over a root and made a noise. We got down and kept still. Miss Watson's big servant, named Jim, was sitting in the kitchen door. He got up and stretched, listening. Then he says, "Who's there?"

He listened some more. Then he come tip-toeing down and stood right between us. We could've touched him, nearly. It was minutes and minutes before anyone made a sound. There was a place on my ankle that got to itching, but I didn't dare scratch it. Then my ear began to itch, and next my back. If you are anywheres where it won't do for you to scratch, why you will itch all over. Pretty soon Jim says, "Say—who is you? Where is you?

Dog my cats[1] if I didn't hear something. I'll just set down here and listen till I hear it again."

So he sat down on the ground between me and Tom. He leaned back against a tree and stretched his legs out till one of them almost touched one of mine. I began to itch all over again. I **reckoned**[2] I couldn't stand it a minute longer. Just then Jim begun to breathe heavy. Next he begun to **snore.**[3]

Tom made a sign to me, and we crept away on our hands and knees. When we was ten foot off, Tom said he wanted to play a joke on old Jim. I thought it was risky, but Tom wanted to try, so we went inside and got three candles. Tom laid five cents on the table for pay. Then we got out. Tom crawled over to where Jim was. When he came back, we took the path that went up the hill on the side of the house. Tom said he'd taken Jim's hat off his head and hung it in a tree. Afterwards Jim said the witches put him in a **trance,**[4] and they rode on his back all over the State. Then they set him under the trees again and hung his hat on a limb. Next time Jim told it, they rode him down to New Orleans. By and by[5] he said they rode him all

---

[1] Dog my cats—an expression of surprise.

[2] **reckoned**—figured or guessed.

[3] **snore**—harsh snorting noises made during sleep.

[4] **trance**—a state something like sleep when people are not completely aware of their surroundings, but seem awake.

[5] By and by—eventually or in awhile.

over the world. He said he even got saddle sores[6] on his back. Jim was proud of his story, and the other slaves would come from miles to hear him tell it.

Well, when Tom and me got to the edge of the hilltop, the stars over us was sparkling ever so fine. Down by the village was the river, awful still and grand. We went down the hill and found Joe Harper, Ben Rogers, and two or three more of the boys. So we took a **skiff**[7] and went down the river, to the big scar[8] on the hillside. That's where we went ashore.

"Now we'll start this band of robbers. We'll call it Tom Sawyer's Gang."

We went into the bushes. Tom made everybody swear to keep the secret. Then he showed them a hole in the hill. We lit the candles and crawled in on our hands and knees. About two hundred yards in, the cave opened up. We got into a kind of room, all damp and cold. Tom says:

"Now we'll start this band of robbers. We'll call it Tom Sawyer's Gang. Everybody that wants to

---

[6] saddle sores—blisters where a saddle rubs against the skin of a horse.

[7] **skiff**—small, light boat for rowing.

[8] scar—mark.

join has to take an **oath,**[9] and write his name in blood."

Everybody said they would. So Tom read the oath. It swore every boy to stick to the band. If anybody done anything to any boy in the band, the gang would kill that person and his family. And if anybody that belonged to the band told the secrets, he must have his throat cut. Then he would be burnt up and the ashes scattered all around. The gang would never mention him again. He would be forgot, forever.

Everybody said it was a real good oath. They asked Tom if he got it out of his own head. He said, some of it, but the rest was out of pirate books and robber books.

Some thought it would be good to kill the families of boys that told the secrets. Tom said it was a good idea, so he took a pencil and wrote it in. Then Ben Rogers says:

"Huck Finn ain't got no family. What you going to do 'bout him?"

"Well, ain't he got a father?" says Tom Sawyer.

"Yes, he's got a father, but you can't never find him. He ain't been seen in these parts for a year or more."

---

[9] **oath**—promise.

They talked it over, and they was going to rule me out. I was almost ready to cry, but all at once I thought of a way out. I offered them Miss Watson. They could kill her. Everybody said:

"Oh, she'll do, she'll do. Huck can come in."

Then they all struck a pin in their fingers to get blood to sign with.

"Now, says Ben Rogers, "what does this gang do?"

"Nothing but robbery and murder," Tom said.

"But who are we going to rob?"

"We stop **stagecoaches**[10] on the road. We kill the people and take their watches and money."

"Must we always kill the people?"

"Oh, sure. It's best. Except some that you bring to the cave here and keep them till they're **ransomed.**"[11]

"Ransomed? What's that?"

"I don't know. But that's what they do. I've seen it in books."

"Now," says Ben Rogers, "what does this gang do?"

—

"Nothing but robbery and murder," Tom said.

---

[10] **stagecoaches**—buggies or coaches pulled by horses that carry passengers.
[11] **ransomed**—held captive until someone pays for the prisoner's release.

"But how can we do it if we don't know what it is?"

"Why, we've got to do it. Do you want to start doing different from what's in the books?"

"Oh, that's all very fine to say, Tom Sawyer. But how in the nation are we going to ransom them if we don't know how to do it? Now what do you think it means?"

"Well I don't know. But maybe if we keep them till they're ransomed, it means that we keep them till they're dead."

"Now, why couldn't you say that before? We'll keep them till they're ransomed to death."

"Say, do we kill the women too?"

"Kill the women? No. You fetch them to the cave, and you're always as polite as pie to them. Then they fall in love with you and never want to go home anymore."

"Well, if that's the way it is, the cave will be so full of women and guys waiting to be ransomed, there won't be no place for the robbers."

Little Tommy Barnes was asleep. When we waked him up, he was scared. He cried and said he wanted to go home, so we said we would all go home and meet next week.

Ben Rogers said he could only get out on Sundays, but all the boys said it would be wicked to rob and kill on Sunday. They agreed to fix a day as soon as they could, and so we started home.

I climbed up the shed and crept into my window just before daybreak. My clothes was all dirty, and I was dog-tired.

CHAPTER THREE

Well, I got a good going-over in the morning from old Miss Watson. But the widow, she didn't **scold.**[1] She only cleaned off the **grease**[2] and clay. She looked so sad that I thought I might behave awhile, if I could. Then Miss Watson took me in the **closet**[3] and prayed, but nothing came of it. She told me to pray every day, and whatever I asked for, I would get it, but it wasn't so. I tried it. Once I got a fish-line but no hooks. It wasn't any good to me without hooks. I tried for the hooks three or four times, but somehow I couldn't make it work.

I went to the woods and thought about it. I says to myself, if a body can get anything they pray for, why can't the widow get back her silver box

---

[1] **scold**—find fault with or blame with angry, harsh words.

[2] **grease**—oily dirt.

[3] **closet**—small room used to store for towels, supplies, clothes, etc.

that was stole? Why can't Miss Watson fatten up? I went and asked the widow about it. She said the thing a body could get by praying was "spiritual gifts." She told me what she meant. I must help other people. I must do everything I could for them. I must never think about myself. Well, I couldn't see nothing good that could come of it, except for the other people. So I didn't worry about it any more, but just let it go.

> **I didn't want to see him no more. He used to always whip me whenever he could get his hands on me.**

Pap hadn't been seen for more than a year, and that was fine with me. I didn't want to see him no more. He used to always whip me whenever he could get his hands on me. That's why I used to head for the woods when he was around. Well, about this time he was found in the river drowned. They thought it was him, anyway. This drowned man was just his size. He had ragged clothes and long hair, just like Pap. Yet they couldn't tell from the face, because it had been in the water so long. They said he was floating on his back in the water. They took him and buried him on the bank, but I knowed mighty well that a drowned man don't float on his back, but on his face. So I knowed, then, that this weren't Pap, but a woman dressed up in a man's clothes. So I feared the old man would turn up again by and by.

We played robbers for a month, and then I left the gang. All the boys did. We hadn't robbed nobody. We hadn't killed any people, but only just pretended. We used to hop out of the woods and go charging down on **hog drovers**[4] and women carrying food in carts. Tom Sawyer called the hogs **"ingots,"**[5] and he called the **turnips**[6] and stuff "jewels." One time Tom said he got secret news that a big group of Spanish salesmen and rich Arabs was going to camp in Cave Hollow. They would bring two hundred elephants, six hundred **camels,**[7] a thousand mules and a load of diamonds. He said we could hide and wait for them, then rush in and kill them and take their things. I didn't believe we could fight such a crowd, but I wanted to see the camels and elephants, so I came along the next day. It turns out, it was only a Sunday-school

---

[4] **hog drovers**—people moving hogs from one place to another.

[5] **ingots**—brick-shaped pieces of cast metal such as gold.

[6] **turnips**—plants with yellow or white roots that are eaten as food.

[7] **camels**—humped, long-necked animals used to carry things, especially across deserts.

picnic, and only a **primer**[8] class at that. We chased the children, but we never got anything but **doughnuts**[9] and jam, a rag doll, and a hymn book. Then the teacher came and made us drop everything. I didn't see no diamonds and I told Tom Sawyer so. He said there was loads of them. He said there was Arabs there too, and elephants and things. I said, why couldn't we see them, then? He said it was all done by magic. He said that some magicians called genies turned the whole thing into a Sunday-school party, just out of spite.

I thought this was only just one of Tom Sawyer's lies. He believed in the Arabs and the elephants, but I think different. To me, it had all the marks of a Sunday-school.

---

[8] **primer**—beginner or first-grade level.

[9] **doughnuts**—small, ring-shaped cakes made of rich light dough fried in deep fat.

CHAPTER FOUR

Three or four months went by, and it was well into the winter now. I had been to school most all the time. Now I could spell, and read, and write just a little. I could even do some math.

At first I hated school. Yet the longer I went to school, the easier it got to be. I was getting used to the widow's ways, too. Living in a house made me **nervous.**[1] Before the cold weather I used to go sleep in the woods. I liked the old ways best, but I was getting so I liked the new ones too, a little bit. The widow said she weren't ashamed of me.

One morning I spilled some salt at breakfast. I reached for some of it to throw over my left shoulder and keep off the bad luck. But that weren't enough to keep off the bad luck. I went down to the

---

[1] **nervous**—jumpy, not at ease, jittery.

front garden. There was an inch of new snow on the ground, and I seen somebody's tracks. They had come up from the **quarry**[2] and stood around awhile, and then went on around the fence. There was a cross in the left boot heel, made with big nails, to keep off the devil.

I ran down the hill, even though I didn't see nobody. I was at Judge Thatcher's as quick as I could get there. He said:

"Why, my boy, you are all out of breath. Did you come for your **interest?**"[3]

"No sir," I says. "Is there some for me?"

> **"I don't want it at all. I want you to take all my money."**

"Oh, yes. Over a hundred and fifty dollars. You better let me invest it along with your six thousand. If you take it, you'll spend it."

"No sir," I says, "I don't want to spend it. I don't want it at all. I want you to take all my money."

He looked surprised.

I says, "You'll take it, won't you?"

---

[2] **quarry**—place where stone or slate is mined or excavated.

[3] **interest**—money added to savings, as a bonus for keeping it in the bank.

He thought awhile, and then he says, "Oh, I see. You want to sell all your property to me, not give it."

Then he wrote something on a paper. He said, "That means I have bought it and paid you for it. Here's a dollar for you. Now, you sign it."

So I signed it, and left.

Miss Watson's servant, Jim, had a hair ball as big as your fist. It had come from the stomach of an ox. Jim used to do magic with it. He said there was a spirit inside of it, and it knowed everything. So I went to him that night. I told him my Pap was here again, for I saw his tracks in the snow. I wanted to know what he was going to do, and where he was going to stay. Jim got out his hair ball, and said something over it. Then he held it up and dropped it on the floor. It fell pretty solid, and only rolled about an inch. Jim tried it again. It acted just the same. He said sometimes it wouldn't talk without money. I told him I had an old slick **counterfeit**[4] quarter that weren't no good. Jim smelled it, bit it, rubbed it, and said he would make the hair ball think it was good. He put the quarter under

---

[4] **counterfeit**—fake.

the hair ball, then got down and listened again. This time he said the hair ball would tell my whole **fortune.**[5]

"Your old father don't know yet what he's going to do," said Jim. "The best way is to let the old man choose his own way. There's two angels above him. One of them is good and the other one is mean. The good one gets him to go right a little while, then the other comes along. A body can't tell yet which one's going to get him in the end. But you're all right, at least. You'll have trouble in your life and also joy. But you want to keep away from the water. That's where your risks lie."

I lit my candle and went up to my room. There sat Pap, his own self!

---

[5] **fortune**—fate, or the way one's life will turn out.

CHAPTER FIVE

I had shut the door when I turned around and saw him. I used to be scared of him because he beat me so much. But now I thought he weren't worth worrying about. He was almost fifty, and he looked it. His hair was long and greasy. It hung down in front, and his eyes peeped through like he was behind vines. It was all black hair, not gray. There weren't no color in his face. It was white. It was not like another man's white, but a tree-toad white, a fish-belly white. His clothes were just old rags. He had one leg resting on the other knee. The boot on that foot was busted, and two of his toes stuck out. His hat had the top caved in, like a lid.

I stood looking at him. He sat there looking at me. I noticed the window was up, so he had climbed in by the shed. By and by he says, "Nice clothes— very. You think you're a big deal, don't you?"

"Maybe I am, maybe I ain't," I says.

"Don't you give me none of your lip," says he. "You've put on **frills**[1] since I been away. I'll take you down a peg[2] before I get done with you. They say you can read and write. You think you're better than your father now, don't you, because he can't? Who told you to take up such foolishness?"

"The widow. She told me."

"The widow, hey? And who told the widow she could dig into a thing that ain't none of her business?"

"Nobody never told her."

"Well, I'll learn her how to **meddle**.[3] And look here, you drop that school you hear? Your mother couldn't read and write before she died. None of the family could before they died. I can't. And here you're swelling yourself up like this. I won't have it. If I catch you about that school, I'll **tan**[4] you good. First thing you know, you'll get religion, too. I never seen such a son."

---

[1] **frills**—extra touches to make something fancier.

[2] take you down a peg—to humble someone.

[3] **meddle**—interfere or get involved in someone else's business.

[4] **tan**—to beat repeatedly with a whip.

He sat there mumbling and growling a minute, and then he says, "They say you're rich. How's that?"

"They lie, that's how."

"Look here, mind how you talk to me. Don't give me no **sass.**[5] I've been in town two days, and I ain't heard people talk about nothing but you being rich. I heard it way down the river too. That's why I come. You get me that money tomorrow. I want it."

"I ain't got no money."

"You get me that money tomorrow. I want it."

"It's a lie. Judge Thatcher's got it. You get it. I want it."

"I ain't got no money, I tell you. Ask Judge Thatcher. He'll tell you the same."

"All right, I'll ask him. Say, how much you got in your pocket? I want it."

"I only got a dollar."

He took it and bit it[6] to see if it was good. Then he said he was going downtown to get some whisky. When he had got out on the shed, he put his head in again, and told me he was going to watch me. He said he would beat me if I didn't drop out of school.

---

[5] **sass**—back talk.

[6] **bit it**—Pap bites into the coin to see if it is real and made of soft metal.

Next day he was drunk. He went to Judge Thatcher's and tried to make him give up the money, but he couldn't. Then he swore he'd make the law force him.

Judge Thatcher and the widow Douglas went to court to take me away from him. They wanted me to live with one of them for good. However, it was a new judge that had just come to town, and he didn't know the old man. He said courts must not keep families apart. So Judge Thatcher and the widow had to quit trying.

He said he'd whip me till I was black and blue if I didn't raise some money for him.

That pleased the old man. He said he'd whip me till I was black and blue if I didn't raise some money for him. I asked Judge Thatcher for three dollars. Pap took it and got drunk. And he went cussing and whooping all over town till almost midnight. Then they jailed him for a week. But he said he was happy because he was the boss of his son.

When Pap got out of jail, the new judge said he was going to make a man out of him. So he took Pap to his own house and dressed him up clean and nice. After supper he talked to him about not drinking. The old man cried. He said he'd been a fool all his life. Now he was going to be a man nobody would be ashamed of. He hoped the judge would help him and not look down on him. The judge said he could hug him for them words. So he cried, and his wife cried. And when it was bedtime, everyone shook hands with Pap, and the judge's wife kissed his hand. Then they tucked the old man into a nice room.

Some time in the night, Pap got very thirsty. He climbed out onto the porch roof and slid down it. He traded his new coat for a jug and climbed back again. Toward dawn, he crawled out again, drunk, and rolled off the porch. He broke his left arm in two places. He almost froze to death before someone found him.

The judge felt kind of mad. He said maybe somebody could **reform**[7] the old man with a shotgun, but he didn't know no other way.

---

[7] **reform**—improve by removing one's faults.

CHAPTER SIX

Well, pretty soon the old man was up and around again. Then he went for Judge Thatcher in the courts, to make him give up that money. Then he went for me, too, for not stopping school. He catched me a couple of times and **thrashed**[1] me, but I went to school anyway, and outran him most of the time. Every time he got money, he got drunk. Every time he got drunk, he made trouble around town. Every time he made trouble, he got jailed.

He hung around the widow's too much. She told him to stop it. Well, was he ever mad! He said he would show who was Huck Finn's boss. So he watched for me one day and caught me. He took me up the river about three miles in a skiff. He

[1] **thrashed**—beat.

crossed over to the Illinois shore. It was wooded, and there weren't no houses but an old log hut. The timber was so thick you could hardly find the place.

He kept me with him all the time. We lived in that old cabin, and he always locked the door and put the key under his pillow at night. He had a gun, so we fished and hunted, and that was what we lived on. Sometimes he locked me in and went down to the store, where he traded fish and **game**[2] for whisky. When he came home, he got drunk and whipped me. The widow found out where we were. She sent a man over to get me out, but Pap chased him off with the gun.

It was kind of lazy just fishing all day with no books to study. Two months went by and my clothes got to be all rags and dirt. I didn't see how I'd ever got to like it so well at the widow's place. There you had to wash, and eat on a plate, and comb your hair, and go to bed on time.

But by and by, Pap whipped me too much, and I couldn't stand it. I had **welts**[3] all over. He also went away too much, and left me locked inside. Once he locked me in and was gone three days. I was so lonely, I made up my mind I would leave. I had

---

[2] **game**—wild animals hunted for food.

[3] **welts**—ridges raised on the flesh, usually caused by a heavy blow.

tried to get out of that cabin, but I couldn't find no way. But this time I found an old rusty wood saw laid between a **rafter**[4] and the roof. An old blanket was nailed against the logs at the end of the cabin. It kept the wind from blowing through the cracks and putting the candle out. I raised the blanket and cut a part of the bottom log out. I was almost through when I heard Pap's gun in the woods. I dropped the blanket and hid my saw. Pretty soon Pap come in.

Pap weren't in a good humor, so he was himself. He said everything was going wrong. His lawyer said he could win his lawsuit if they ever held the trial. Judge Thatcher knew how to keep putting it off. And he said there'd be another trial to get me away from him. The lawyer thought it would win, this time. This shook me up because I didn't want to go back to the widow's and be so cramped up. He said if they tried to come and get me, he'd take me off to where they could hunt till they dropped and never find me. That made me pretty mad again. I decided I wouldn't stay till he got that chance.

The old man made me go to the boat and get the things he had brought. There was a fifty-pound sack of **cornmeal**,[5] bacon, bullets, whisky, books,

---

[4] **rafter**—plank across a ceiling that supports the walls and roof.
[5] **cornmeal**—food made from corn ground into small pieces.

and other stuff. I carried up a load and then went back down to rest. I thought it all over. I would run away. I could take the gun and some fishing lines and live in the woods. I would get so far away that the old man and the widow could never find me. I would saw out the hole and leave that night, if Pap got drunk enough.

I got all the things up to the cabin. While I was cooking supper the old man took a swig or two and got sort of warmed up. He had been drunk over in town and laid in the gutter all night, and he was a sight to look at. Whenever his liquor begun to work, he talked about the government. This time he says:

"Call this a government! Why, just look at it. Here's the law standing ready to take a man's son away from him. Yes, just as that man has got that son raised at last, and ready to go to work and begin to do something for him, the law goes for him. And the law takes a man worth six thousand dollars and jams him into an old cabin like this. And it lets him go around in clothes that ain't fit for a hog. They call that a government!"

Pap was a-going on so, he never noticed where his old legs was taking him, so he fell over a tub of pork. He hopped around on one leg and then on the other. At last he kicked the tub in anger. It wasn't a good idea, because that was the boot that had two toes leaking out in front. So now he howled. He fell down, rolled around and held his toes.

After supper Pap took up the jug again. I thought he would be blind drunk in about an hour. Then I would steal the key or saw myself out. He drank and drank and fell down onto his blankets, but luck didn't run my way. He groaned and moaned for a long time. I couldn't keep my eyes open, and so before I knowed it, I was sound asleep.

All of a sudden there was an awful scream, and I was up. There was Pap, skipping around every which way, yelling about snakes. He said they was crawling up his legs. Pretty soon he fell down and rolled over and over. He kicked and hit at the air, saying devils had ahold of him. He begged them to let him alone. Then he rolled up in his blanket and began crying.

By and by he jumped up on his feet, looking wild. He chased me around with a knife, calling me the Angel of Death. He said he would kill me so I couldn't come for him no more. I told him I was only Huck, but he laughed and kept on chasing me. Pretty soon he was all tired out, and dropped down with his back against the door. He said he would rest a minute and then kill me.

So he dozed off pretty soon. I quietly got down the gun. I made sure it was loaded. Then I pointed it toward Pap and sat down to wait.

CHAPTER SEVEN

"Get up!"

I opened my eyes and looked around. It was after sun-up, and I had been sound asleep. Pap was standing over me, looking sick. He says, "What you doing with this gun?"

I figured he didn't know what he had been doing all night. I says, "Somebody tried to get in, so I was waiting for him."

"Why didn't you wake me up?"

"Well, I tried to, but I couldn't. I couldn't budge you."

"Well, all right. Don't stand there all day. Go out and see if there's a fish on the lines for breakfast. I'll be along in a minute."

He unlocked the door and I went up the riverbank. I kept an eye out for what the river might bring. Well, all at once, here comes a canoe. I jumped head-first off the bank, like a frog, clothes on and all. I swam out to the canoe, climbed in, and paddled her ashore. Thinks I, the old man will be glad when he sees this. She's worth ten dollars. But when I got to shore, I had an idea. I'd hide her good. Then, instead of walking through the woods when I run away, I'd go down the river about fifty miles. I'd camp in one place for good instead of tramping on foot.

I got her hid in a bunch of **willows.**[1] Then I saw the old man down the path a ways. He scolded me for being so slow, but I told him I fell in the river. Otherwise, I knowed he would ask why I was wet. We got five catfish off the lines and went home.

He thought about that morning and said, "Next time a man comes a-prowling[2] around here, you wake me up, you hear? I would've shot him." Then he took a nap, while I sat there thinking. I says to myself, I can fix it now so nobody will think of following me.

About twelve o'clock we went down to the bank. The river was coming up pretty fast, with lots of **driftwood**[3] going by on the rise. By and by,

---

[1] **willows**—trees with long narrow leaves and soft, bendable branches that hang low to the ground.

[2] a-prowling—roaming or wandering.

[3] **driftwood**—loose logs floating on the water.

along comes nine logs fastened together. We went out with the skiff and towed the raft ashore. Then we had dinner. Anybody but Pap would've waited to catch more stuff, but that weren't Pap's style. Nine logs was enough. He must shove off and go to town and sell. So he locked me in the cabin and took the skiff and started towing the raft at half-past three. I waited till he had a good start, then I got out my saw and went to work cutting the hole again. Before he made it to the other side of the river, I was out of the cabin.

I took the sack of cornmeal to where the canoe was hid and put it in there. Then I done the same with the bacon. I also took a bucket, a tin cup, my saw, two blankets, the pan, fishing lines, matches and everything else worth a cent. I fetched the gun down. Then I covered my tracks with dirt. I put the log back in the cabin wall and leaned rocks to hold it there. If you didn't know it was sawed, you would never notice it back there.

I took the gun and went up a piece[4] into the woods. I was hunting around for some birds when I saw a wild pig. Hogs soon went wild when they

---

[4] a piece—informal phrase that means "a ways."

got away from the farmers. I shot this one and took him into camp.

Next I took the axe and smashed in the door. I **fetched**[5] the pig and took him in to the table. I cut his throat with a knife and laid him on the ground to bleed. Then I took an old sack and put a lot of big rocks in it. I dragged it to the door and through the woods, down into the river. I dumped it in, and down it sunk, out of sight. You could see that something had been dragged over the ground. I did wish Tom Sawyer was there. I knowed he would throw in the fancy touches.

> *I did wish Tom Sawyer was there. I knowed he would throw in the fancy touches.*

Well, at last I pulled out some of my hair. I put the pig's blood and my hair on the ax. Then I took up the pig and held him to my chest with my jacket, so he couldn't drip. I dumped him in the river. Then I thought of one more thing. I got the bag of cornmeal and cut a hole in it. I carried it out past the house in the other direction, toward a lake. I let the cornmeal leak out in a trail. At the shore, I tied the bag up so it wouldn't leak any more. I took it and my saw to the boat again on the river side.

---

[5] **fetched**—went and got, brought.

It was about dark, now, so I hid the boat down the river and waited for the moon to rise. I took a bite to eat, and then lied down in the canoe. I says to myself, they'll follow the track of that sack of rocks to the shore. Then they'll drag the river for me. They'll try to find the robbers that killed me and took the things. They won't ever hunt the river for anything but my dead **carcass.**[6] And they'll soon get tired of that, so I can stay anywhere I want to. Jackson's Island is good enough for me. Nobody ever comes there.

I was pretty tired, and the first thing I knowed, I was asleep. When I woke up, I didn't know where I was. I sat up and looked around, a little scared. Then I remembered. The river looked miles and miles across. The moon was so bright I could count the drift logs that went by. Everything was dead quiet. It looked late. It *smelled* late. You know what I mean. I don't know the words to put it in.

Pretty soon I heard a sound away over the water. It was that dull sound that comes from oars working at night. I peeped out through the branches, and there it was—a skiff boat, away across the water. When it came near me, I seen there weren't but one man in it. Thinks I, maybe it's Pap. He went

---

[6] **carcass**—body (usually the dead body of an animal being prepared for eating).

by so close I could've reached out the gun and touched him. Well, it sure was Pap. He looked sober too, the way he worked those oars so fast.

I didn't lose no time. I went downstream soft but quick in the shade of the bank. I made two miles and a half, and then struck out to the middle of the river. Pretty soon I would pass the ferry landing and people might see me. I got out among the driftwood and then lied down in the bottom of the boat and let her float. I had a good rest looking away into the sky, not a cloud in it. I heard people laughing and joking at the ferry landing. Soon the talk got so far away, I couldn't make out the words any more.

I was way below the **ferry**[7] now. I rose up and there was Jackson's Island. It stood in the river, big and dark, like a steamboat with no lights. I landed on the side towards the Illinois shore. I run the canoe into a deep dent in the bank. I would have to part the tree branches to get in and out. Nobody could've seen the boat from the outside. There was a little gray in the sky, now, so I stepped into the woods and took a nap before breakfast.

---

[7] **ferry**—boat that carries people, vehicles, and goods back and forth (as across a river).

CHAPTER EIGHT

The sun was up high when I waked. I lied there in the grass, thinking and feeling rested. I could see the sun through the big trees all around. There was freckled places on the ground where the light shifted down through the leaves. Two squirrels set on a limb and talked at me very friendly.

I felt lazy. I didn't want to get up and cook breakfast. Well, I was dozing off again when I hear a deep sound of "boom!" up the river. I hopped up and looked out at a hole in the leaves. I seen smoke laying on the water. And there was the ferry boat full of people. I knowed what was the matter, now. You see, they was firing the cannon over the water, trying to make my carcass come to the top. I set there and watched. I was having a good time seeing them hunt for my **remainders,**[1] if I only had a bit to

---

[1] **remainders**—Huck's slang word for "remains."

eat. Well, I happened to think how they always put **quicksilver**[2] in loaves of bread and float them off. The loaves go right to the drowned body and stop there. So says I, I'll keep a lookout. I changed to the other edge of the island, to see what luck I could have. A big loaf came along. I almost got it with a long stick, but my foot slipped. By and by along comes another one, and this time I won. I took out the plug and shook out the little dab of silver and ate the bread. It was good baker's bread, not your low-down corn pone.[3] I reckon the widow or the **parson**[4] or somebody prayed that this bread would find me. So maybe it works when the widow or the parson prays, but it don't work for me.

By and by the ferry boat come along. She drifted in so close that they could've run out a **plank**[5] and walked ashore. Most everybody was on the boat. Pap, Judge Thatcher, Tom Sawyer, his old Aunt Polly, Sid and Mary, and plenty more. Everybody was talking about the murder. The captain broke in and says, "Look sharp, now. Maybe he washed ashore. I hope so anyway."

I didn't hope so. They all crowded up and leaned over the rails, watching with all their might.

---

[2] **quicksilver**—mercury, which looks like liquid silver.

[3] corn pone—cornbread made without milk or eggs.

[4] **parson**—minister.

[5] **plank**—a piece of wood or lumber often used to board ships.

I could see them, but they couldn't see me. Then the captain sung out, "Stand away!" and the cannon let off such a blast that it made me deaf with the noise and blind with the smoke. The boat floated on and went out of sight. I could hear the booming, now and then, but after an hour, I didn't hear it no more.

I knowed I was all right now. Nobody else would come hunting after me. I got my traps out of the canoe and made me a nice camp in the thick woods. I made a kind of tent out of my blankets to put my things under. When it was dark, I set by my campfire feeling pretty good, but by and by it got sort of **lonesome.**[6] I set on the bank and listened to the waves and counted the stars. Then I went to bed.

And so it went for three days and nights. But the next day I explored the island. I found strawberries, green grapes, raspberries, and blackberries. They would all come in handy, I guessed.

That night, I slid out from shore and rowed over to the Illinois bank. I went out in the woods and cooked a supper. I thought I might stay there

---

[6] **lonesome**—feeling low or sad because one is all alone or without friends.

all night. Suddenly I heard a *plunkety plunk, plunkety-plunk.* I says to myself, horses coming. Next I hear people's voices. I got everything into the boat as quick as I could. I heard a man say, "We better camp here. The horses is about beat out."

I left quickly. I went back to the old place and slept in the boat. But I didn't sleep much. By and by I says to myself, I can't live this way. I'm going to find out who's here on the island with me.

So I rowed back over there. I let the canoe drop among the shadows. Then I got my gun and slipped out into the woods, to find that campfire. Soon I saw a fire through the trees. I got close enough to look, and there laid a man on the ground. He had a blanket around his head. I kept my eyes on him. Daylight was coming. Pretty soon he stretched and threw off the blanket. It was Miss Watson's servant Jim! I was so glad to see him.

"Don't hurt me! I ain't ever done harm to a ghost. I always liked dead people."

"Hello, Jim!" I said and skipped out.

He stood up and stared at me. Then he dropped to his knees and put his hands together. He says, "Don't hurt me! I ain't ever done harm to a ghost. I always liked dead people. You go get in the river again, where you belong. Don't do nothing to old Jim, who was always your friend."

Well, I told him I weren't dead. I was ever so glad to see Jim. I weren't alone now.

"How long you been on the island, Jim?" I asked.

"I come the night after you was killed. I been living on strawberries ever since."

> **"How long you been on the island, Jim?" I asked.**
>
> —
>
> **"I come the night after you was killed. I been living on strawberries ever since."**

"Well, you must be starved, ain't you?"

"I reckon I could eat a horse. How long you been on the island?"

"Since the night I got killed."

We went over to where the boat was. While he built a fire, I got corn meal, bacon, coffee, cups and sugar. Jim thought it was all done by magic. I catched a good big catfish. Jim cleaned him and fried him.

When breakfast was ready, we sat on the grass and ate. We got pretty stuffed. By and by Jim says, "Huck, who was it that was killed in that **shanty**,[7] if it weren't you?"

---

[7] **shanty**—shack or crude cabin.

Then I told him the whole story, and he said it was smart. He said Tom Sawyer couldn't have thought up a better plan that what I had. Then I says, "How do you come to be here, Jim?"

He said, "Maybe I better not tell."

"Why, Jim?"

"Well, there's reasons. But you wouldn't tell on me if I was to tell you, would you, Huck?"

"Darned if I would, Jim."

"Well, Huck, I *run off*."

"Jim!"

"You said you wouldn't tell."

"Well, I did, and I'll stick to it. So now tell me all about it."

"Well, you see, it was this way. Old Miss Watson, she picks on me all the time. But she always said she wouldn't sell me down to Orleans. But I noticed there was a slave trader around the place lately. Well, one night I hear old Miss Watson tell the widow she's going to sell me. She didn't want to, but she could get eight hundred dollars for me. It was such a big stack of money, she had to do it. The widow, she tried to get her to say she wouldn't do it. I never waited to hear the rest. I ran off mighty quick, I tell you. I took off down the hill and looked for a boat, but there was too many people around. Everybody was talking about how your Pap come to town and said you was killed. By the talk, I got to know all about the killing. I was awful sorry, Huck, but I ain't no more."

"Then what did you do?"

"I looked for a raft in the river. I swam out real quiet and got up on the end of it. The men in the middle didn't see me. I hoped I could ride twenty-five miles before daylight. But I didn't have no luck. A man begin to walk toward me. So I jumped off and swam to this island."

Some young birds come along, flying a yard or two at a time and landing. Jim said it was a sign it was going to rain. Jim knowed all kinds of signs. He said he knowed most everything. I said it looked like all the signs was about bad luck. I asked him if there weren't any good-luck signs. He says:

"Mighty few. If you got hairy arms and a hairy chest, it's a sign that you're going to be rich."

"Have you got hairy arms and a hairy chest, Jim?"

"Don't you see I have?"

"Well, are you rich?"

"No, but I been rich once and going to be rich again. Once I had fourteen dollars, but I took to **speculating.**"[8]

"What did you speculate in, Jim?"

"Stock."

"What kind of stock?"

"Why, livestock. Cattle, you know. I put ten dollars in a cow. But the cow up and died."

"So you lost the ten dollars."

"I only lost nine of it. I sold the hide and **tallow**[9] for a dollar and ten cents."

"Did you speculate any more?"

"Yes. You know Mr. Bradish's one-legged servant? Well, he started a bank. He says anybody that puts in a dollar would get four dollars more at the end of the year. Well, all of us slaves went in, but I was the only one that had much. Then I thought I'd invest the thirty-five dollars he owed me, to keep things moving. There was a slave named Bob that catched a wood flat. I bought it off him and told him to take his thirty-five dollars at the end of the year. But somebody stole the wood-flat that night. The next day, the one-legged slave say the bank's busted. I had only ten cents left."

---

[8] **speculating**—to buy and then sell goods or stocks at a risk, hoping for a profit.

[9] **tallow**—animal fat used to make candles or soap.

"What did you do with it?"

"I had a dream that I should give it to a slave named Balum. He's lucky, they say. The dream say let Balum invest the ten cents, and he'd make it grow. Well, Balum, he took the money and then went to church. The preacher said that whoever gives to the poor lends to the Lord and will get his money back a hundred times. So Balum give the ten cents to the poor and waited to see what would come back."

"Well, what came of it, Jim?"

"Nothing. I couldn't get that money back. Balum, he couldn't either. Bound to get your money back a hundred times, the preacher says! If I could get the ten cents back, I'd call it fair."

"Well, it's all right, Jim. You're going to be rich again some time or other."

"Yes, and I'm rich now, come to think of it. I own myself, and I'm worth eight hundred dollars. I wish I had *that* money."

CHAPTER NINE

I wanted to go and look at a place that I'd found when I was exploring. We started and soon got to it, because the island was only three miles long and a quarter of a mile wide.

This place was a long steep hill. We had a rough time getting to the top, because the bushes were so thick. We found a good big **cavern**[1] in the rock. The cavern was as big as two or three rooms, and Jim could stand up straight in it.

Jim said we should hide the boat and put all the traps in the cavern, we could rush there if anybody came to the island. And besides, he said, the little birds knew it was going to rain soon. So we went back and carried all the traps up there.

The door of the cavern was big enough to roll a hog's head in. On one side of the door, the floor

---

[1] **cavern**—cave.

stuck out a little bit. It was flat and a good place to build a fire. So we built it there and cooked dinner. We spread the blankets inside for a carpet. Pretty soon it began to thunder and lightning. I never seen such wind and rain. It got so dark that it looked all blue-black outside, and lovely. The trees looked dim and spider-webby.

"Jim, this is nice," I says. "I wouldn't want to be nowhere else but here. Pass me another hunk of fish and some hot cornbread."

"Well, you wouldn't be here if it hadn't been for Jim. You'd be down in the woods getting drowned. The birds know when it's going to rain, child."

The river went on rising for ten or twelve days. At last it was over the banks. Daytimes we rowed all over the island in the canoe. It was cool and shady in the deep woods. On every broken-down tree, you could see rabbits and snakes and such. We could've had pets enough if we'd wanted them.

One night we catched a little piece of a raft. It was twelve foot wide and about fifteen or sixteen foot long. Another night, when we was up at the head of the island just before daylight, here comes a house floating down the river. She was a two-story, and tilted over. We went out there and got aboard. In at the window, we could see a bed, and a table, and two old chairs, and lots of things around on the floor. There was clothes hanging against the wall. There was something lying on the floor in the far corner that looked like a man.

"Hello, you!" Jim says. But it didn't move. So I yelled again. Then Jim says, "The man ain't asleep. He's dead. You hold still. I'll go and see."

"It's a dead man. Yes, indeed. He's been shot in the back."

He went and looked, and says, "It's a dead man. Yes, indeed. He's been shot in the back. I think he's been dead two or three days. Don't look at his face, Huck. It's too awful."

I didn't look at him at all. Jim threw some old rags over him. Then we looked at what else was on the floor. There were playing cards, old whisky bottles, and two masks made out of black cloth. There were two old dirty **calico**[2] dresses and a sun **bonnet**,[3] and some men's clothing too. We put it all in the canoe. It might come in handy. We got an old tin **lantern**,[4] a lot of candles, an old bed quilt, needles,

---

[2] **calico**—cotton cloth printed with a pattern.

[3] **bonnet**—a girl's or woman's hat with a broad brim that goes around the face.

[4] **lantern**—a light that can be carried.

buttons and some thread. We also found some nails and a fishing line. And so, all around, we made a good **haul.**[5]

When we was ready to leave, it was broad daylight. I made Jim lie down in the boat and cover up with the quilt. If he sat up, people could tell he was a slave. We had no accidents and didn't see nobody. We got home to the cavern safe.

---

[5] **haul**—take, everything collected in a single effort.

CHAPTER TEN

After breakfast, I wanted to talk about the dead man, but Jim didn't want to. He said it would bring bad luck. Besides, he said, the man might come back and haunt us. That sounded likely, so I didn't say no more. We went through the clothes we'd got and found eight dollars sewed up in an overcoat.

"Now, what did you say when I found a snake skin on the ridge day before yesterday?" I asked. "You said it was the worst bad luck in the world. Well, now we raked in all these supplies and eight dollars besides. I wish we could have some bad luck like this every day, Jim."

"Never you mind, honey. It's a-comin'."

It did come too. After lunch Friday, I found a rattlesnake in the cavern. I killed him and put him on Jim's blanket, just for fun. Well, by night, I forgot all about the snake. When Jim lied down in the dark, the snake's mate was there, and bit him.

He jumped up yelling. I struck a light and saw the snake getting ready for another spring. I killed him with a stick, and Jim grabbed Pap's whisky jug and began to pour it down. He was barefooted, and the snake bit him right on the heel. That all comes of my being such a fool. I forgot that when you leave a dead snake, its mate comes and curls around it.

Jim was laid up for four days and nights. His foot swelled up pretty big, and so did his leg. The drink helped, but I'd rather been bit with a snake than to drink Pap's whisky. I made up my mind I wouldn't ever touch a snake skin again.

Jim liked that idea. Then he said, couldn't I dress up like a girl? That was a good idea.

Next morning it was getting slow and dull, and I wanted to stir things up. I thought I would cross the river and find out what was going on. Jim liked that idea. Then he said, couldn't I dress up like a girl? That was a good idea. So we shortened up one of the dresses, and I turned up my pant legs. I put on the sun bonnet and tied it under my chin. Jim said nobody would know me, even in the daytime, hardly. I practiced all day to get used to the things. Jim said I didn't walk like a girl, and he said I must quit pulling up my gown to get at my pants pocket. I tried to do better.

I took the boat across the river just after dark. At the bottom end of town, a light burned in a little hut where no one had lived for a long time. I wondered who had moved in. I went up and peeped in at the window. There was a woman about forty years old, knitting by candlelight. She was a stranger. Now this was lucky, because I was getting afraid. People might know my voice and find me out. But if this woman had been in town even two days, she could probably tell me all I needed to know. I knocked at the door and tried to act like a girl.

CHAPTER ELEVEN

"Come in," says the woman, and I did. "Take a chair."

I done it. She looked me over and says, "What might your name be?"

"Sarah Williams."

"Where abouts do you live? Close by?"

"No, ma'am. In Hookerville, seven miles below. I've walked all the way, and I'm all tired out."

"Hungry, too, I'll bet. I'll find you something."

"No, I ain't hungry. My mother's down sick, and out of money. I come to tell my uncle, Abner Moore. He lives at the upper end of town. Do you know him?"

"No, but I don't know everybody yet. I haven't lived here quite two weeks. It's a long ways to the upper end of town. You better stay here all night. Take off your bonnet."

"No," I says, "I'll rest awhile and go on."

She said she wouldn't let me go by myself. Her husband would be in soon, and she'd send him along with me. Then she got to talking about her family and her moving here and all that she'd heard. She told about me and Tom Sawyer finding the six thousand dollars. She also knew all about Pap. At last she got down to where I was killed.

"Who done it?" I asked.

"Well, I reckon people here would like to know who killed him. Some thinks old Finn done it himself."

"Is that so?"

"Most everybody thought it at first. He'll never know how close he come to getting **lynched**.[1] But before night, they decided it was done by a runaway slave named Jim."

"Why he—" I stopped. I thought I'd better keep still. She went on.

"He run off the very night Huck Finn was killed. So there's a reward out for him—three hundred dollars. And there's a reward out for old Finn too—two hundred dollars. You see, he come to town the morning after the murder and told about it, but then he was gone. Well, next day they found out Jim was gone. He hadn't been seen since

---

[1] **lynched**—hanged.

ten o'clock the night the murder was done. So they put it on him. The next day back comes old Finn. He went crying to Judge Thatcher to get some money to hunt Jim. The judge gave him some, and he got drunk. He stayed around till after midnight, then went off with a couple of mean-looking strangers. Well, he ain't come back since. People think now that he killed his boy and fixed things so folks would think robbers done it. Then he'd get Huck's money without a lawsuit."

> **"People think now that he killed his boy and fixed things so folks would think robbers done it. Then he'd get Huck's money without a lawsuit."**

"Has everybody quit thinking the runaway slave done it?"

"Oh, not everybody. But they'll get him pretty soon, now, and maybe they can scare the truth out of him."

"They're still after him?"

"Of course they are. Do people get the chance for a three-hundred-dollar reward every day? Some folks think he ain't far from here. I'm one of them. A few days ago I was talking with an old couple. They happened to say hardly anybody ever goes to that island over **yonder**[2] that they call Jackson's Island. I done some thinking. I was pretty sure I'd seen smoke over there a day or two before that. I think that slave's hiding over there. My husband's going over to see tonight."

I had got so uneasy I couldn't set still. I had to do something with my hands, so I took up a needle and tried to put the thread through the hole. My hands shook, and I was doing a bad job. The woman looked at me and smiled a little. I put down the needle.

"Three hundred dollars is a lot of money," I said. "I wish my mother could get it. Is your husband going over there tonight?"

"Oh, yes. He went with another man to get a boat and a gun. They'll go after midnight."

"Couldn't they see better in daytime?"

"Yes. And couldn't the runaway see better too? After midnight, he'll be asleep. They can hunt up his camp fire, if he's got one."

"I didn't think of that."

The woman kept looking at me funny. Pretty soon she says, "What did you say your name was, honey?"

"M—Mary Williams."

---

[2] **yonder**—in the distance.

"Honey, I thought you said it was Sarah when you first come in?"

"Oh, yes, I did. Sarah Mary Williams. Sarah's my first name. Some calls me Sarah, some calls me Mary."

The woman fell to talking about how hard times were, and how the rats owned the place. She said she had to have things handy to throw at them. She said she was a good shot but she'd hurt her arm a day or two ago. She watched for a rat and banged away at him but missed him. She said, "Ouch!" Then she told me to try for the next one. The first rat that showed his nose, I let him have it. She said that was first rate. She said, "Keep your eye on the rats. You better have something handy to throw."

So she dropped a lump of lead into my lap, and I clapped my legs on it. Then she looked me in the eyes and says, "Come now, what's your real name?"

"Wh-what, mum?"

"What's your real name? Is it Bill, or Tom, or Bob?"

I shook like a leaf. She said "I ain't going to hurt you, and I ain't going to tell on you. You keep your secret, and trust me. There ain't no harm in running away. You've been treated bad, I suppose. Bless you, child, I wouldn't tell on you. Tell me all about it now."

So I said I would tell her everything. Then I told her my father and mother was dead, and I had to live with a mean old farmer in the country. He treated me so bad, I couldn't stand it. When he went away, I took some of his daughter's old clothes and ran. I believed my uncle Abner Moore would take care of me. That was why I came to this town of Goshen.

"Goshen, child? This ain't Goshen. This is St. Petersburg.[3] Goshen's ten miles up the river. Who told you this was Goshen?"

"Why a man I met this morning. He told me when the roads forked I must take the right side to get to Goshen."

"He was drunk, I guess."

"Well, it ain't no matter now. I got to be moving along. I'll get to Goshen before daylight."

"Hold on a minute. I'll fix you a snack to take along." So she fixed a snack and says, "What's your real name, now?"

"George Peters, mum."

---

[3] Goshen and St. Petersburg are small towns along the Mississippi River.

"Well, try to remember it, George. And don't go around in that old dress. You do a girl pretty poor. The way you hold the thread, the way you throw things at a rat, and the way you catch a lump of lead, why, I spotted you as a boy all along. Now go along to your uncle, Sarah Mary Williams George Peters."

"Get up, Jim! There ain't no time to lose. They're after us!"

I went up the bank and then back to where my boat was. I hurried upstream and started for the island. I took off the sun bonnet, for I didn't want no **blinders**[4] on. When I was in the middle, I heard the clock strike. I stopped and listened. The sound come soft but clear—eleven. When I got to the island, I headed right into the woods where my old camp used to be. I started a good fire there. Then I jumped into the canoe and went to our place, as fast as I could go. I ran through the woods and up the ridge, into the cavern. There Jim laid, sound asleep. I says, "Get up, Jim! There ain't no time to lose. They're after us!"

---

[4] **blinders**—black pieces of cardboard or leather on a bridle fitting over a horse's head to keep the horse looking straight ahead.

Jim never asked no questions. But the way he worked for the next half-hour showed how scared he was. By that time, everything we had in the world was on our raft. We put out the campfire at the cavern. We got on the raft and slipped along down in the shade, past the foot of the island, never saying a word.

CHAPTER TWELVE

It must've been close to one o'clock when we got below the island at last. If the men went to the island, they must've found the campfire I built, and waited all night for Jim to come. Anyways, they stayed away from us.

When the first streak of day begun to show, we tied up the boat to a tow-head. A tow-head is a sand bar thick with cottonwood trees. We cut up some branches from the trees and covered up the raft with them. We laid there all day and watched the rafts and **steamboats**[1] spin down the Missouri shore. We watched the upbound steamboats going up the river against the **current**[2] fight the big river in the middle.

---

[1] **steamboats**—riverboats powered by steam.
[2] **current**—steady flow or movement of a river.

When it began to get dark, we poked our heads out of the cottonwood trees. We floated down the river on the raft. Nothing in sight, so Jim took some of the top planks of the raft and built a snug **wigwam.**[3] So now the blankets and traps was out of the reach of the steamboat waves. We fixed up a short forked stick to hang the old lantern on. We must always light the lantern whenever we see a steamboat coming, to keep from getting run over.

The second night we floated seven or eight hours. The river current moved us along over four miles an hour. We catched fish and talked. We took a swim now and then to stay awake. It was kind of **solemn,**[4] drifting down the big still river, laying on our backs, looking up at the stars. We didn't ever feel like talking or laughing loud.

Every night we passed towns. Some looked like nothing but a shiny bed of lights on the black hillside. The fifth night we passed St. Louis.[5] It was like the whole world lit up. Every night now, I'd go ashore and buy ten or fifteen cents' worth of meal or bacon. Sometimes I lifted a chicken and took

---

[3] **wigwam**—a tent made by fastening skins or mats over a framework of poles.

[4] **solemn**—serious or important; not a light occasion.

[5] St. Louis—city down the Mississippi River from St. Petersburg.

him along. Pap always said, take a chicken when you get a chance, because if you don't want him, you can find somebody that does. I never seen Pap when he didn't want the chicken himself, but that is what he used to say, anyway.

Mornings, before daylight, I slipped into corn-field and "borrowed" a watermelon or pumpkin, or some new corn. Pap always said it weren't no harm to take things, if you was meaning to pay them back sometime. The widow said it weren't anything but a soft name for stealing. Jim said he reckoned the widow was partly right and Pap was partly right. The best way would be for us to pick two or three things from the list and say we wouldn't borrow them any more. Then it wouldn't be no harm to borrow the others. So we talked it over one night and decided to drop crab apples. I was glad the way it come out, too, because crab apples ain't ever good.

The fifth night below St. Louis, we had a big storm. The rain poured down in a solid sheet. We stayed in the wigwam and let the raft take care of itself. When the lightning glared out, we could see a big straight river ahead and high, rocky **bluffs**[6] on both sides. By and by says I, "Jim, look yonder!" It was a steamboat that had killed herself on a rock.

---

[6] **bluffs**—steep cliff or bank along a river.

We was drifting straight down for her. The lightning showed her very clearly. She was leaning over.

Well, it being a stormy night, I felt just the way any other boy would feel. I wanted to get aboard. So I says, "Let's land on her, Jim."

But Jim was against it. He says, "I don't want to go fooling around on no wreck. Likely as not, there's a watchman on that wreck."

"Watchman your grandmother," I says. "There ain't nothing to watch. Do you think anybody's going to risk his life on such a night? The wreck's likely to break up and wash down the river any minute." Jim couldn't say nothing to that, so he didn't try. "And besides," I says, "we might borrow something worth having out of the captain's **stateroom**.[7] Do you reckon Tom Sawyer would ever go by this thing? He'd call it an adventure. He'd land on that wreck if it was his last act."

"Do you reckon Tom Sawyer would ever go by this thing? He'd call it an adventure. He'd land on that wreck if it was his last act."

Jim, he grumbled a little, but then he gave in. We grabbed the **derrick**[8] and fastened the raft. The deck was high out of the water there. We went

---

[7] **stateroom**—private room or bed for a passenger or crew member.

[8] **derrick**—framework for holding machinery or the arm of a crane in place.

sneaking down the slope of it in the dark, feeling our way with our feet. Pretty soon we struck the front end of the skylight and climbed onto it. The next step put us in front of the captain's door, which was open. Down through the hall we saw a light! In the same second, we seemed to hear low voices inside!

Jim whispered that he was feeling mighty sick. He told me to come along. I says, all right, but just then I heard a voice wail out, "Oh please don't, boys. I swear I won't ever tell!"

Another voice said, "It's a lie, Jim Turner. You always want more than your share. You've always got it, too, because you said you'd tell. But this time you've said it just one time too many."

By this time Jim was gone for the raft, but not me. I says to myself, Tom Sawyer wouldn't back out now, and so I won't either. I dropped down on my hands and knees and crept on in the dark. When I passed the last room, I looked in there. I seen a man on the floor, tied hand and foot. Two men stood over him. One of them had a dim lantern in his hand. The other one has a handgun. This one keeps pointing at the man's head on the floor.

The man on the floor was saying, "Please don't, Bill. I ain't ever going to tell." And every time he said that, the man with the lantern would laugh and say, "Indeed you ain't! You ain't going to hurt nobody any more, Jim Turner. Put *up* that pistol, Bill."

Bills says, "I don't want to, Jake Packard. I'm for killing him. Didn't he kill old Hatfield just the same way, and don't he deserve it?"

"But I don't *want* him killed. I've got my reasons."

"Bless your heart for them words, Jack Packard!" Says the man on the floor.

Packard hung up his lantern on a nail and started towards where I was. He motioned Bill to come. I darted as fast as I couldn't, about two yards, but I couldn't make very good time. I crawled into a room on the upper side. The man come a-pawing along in the dark. When Packard got to my state room, he says, "Here. Come in here."

And in they come. Before they got in, I was in the upper **berth,**[9] cornered, and sorry I come. They stood there and talked. I couldn't see them, but I could tell where they was by the whisky they'd been having. I was glad I didn't drink whisky.

Bill wanted to kill Turner. He says, "If we was to give both our shares to him now, it wouldn't

---

[9] **berth**—a bunk in the sleeping area of a boat or train.

matter later. Sure as you're born, he'll turn us in. I'm for putting him out of his troubles."

"So am I," says Packard, very quiet.

"Well, then, let's go and do it."

"Hold on a minute. You listen to me. Shooting's good but there's quieter ways if the thing's got to be done. We'll gather up whatever we've overlooked in the staterooms. We'll put it on the skiff, take it to shore, and hide it all. Then we'll wait. Now I say it ain't going to be more than two hours before this wreck washes off down the river. See? He'll be drowned and won't have nobody to blame for it but his own self. I reckon that's better than killing him. I'm not in favor of killing a man if you can get around it. It ain't good sense. It ain't good morals. Ain't I right?"

"Yes, I reckon you are. But suppose she *don't* break up and wash off?"

"Well, we can wait the two hours anyway, and see."

I says, "Quick, Jim! There's a gang of killers in there."

"All right, then. Come along."

So they walked out, and I ran out of there in a cold sweat. It was dark on deck, but I whispered, "Jim!" He answered up, right at my elbow, with a sort of moan. I says, "Quick, Jim! There's a gang of killers in there. If we don't hunt up their boat and set her drifting down the river, one of 'em will be in a bad fix. But if we find their boat, we can put all of 'em in a bad fix. We can send the Sheriff for 'em. You start the raft and—"

"Raft? There ain't no raft no more. She done broke loose and gone. And here we is."

CHAPTER THIRTEEN

I catched my breath and almost passed out. But it weren't no time to get soft. We had to find that boat now. We had to have it for ourselves! So we went a-quaking and a-shaking down the side of the steamboat. It seemed a week before we got to the back of her. No sign of a boat. Jim said he felt too scared to go any further. But I said we'd be in a fix if we got left on this wreck. So on we prowled again. When we got pretty close to the middle of the boat, there was the skiff, sure enough. I could just barely see her. I felt ever so thankful. In another second I would've been aboard her, but just then the door opened. One of the men stuck his head out. He flung a bag of something into the boat. Then he got in himself. It was Packard. Then Bill come out and got in.

Packard says, in a low voice, "All ready. Shove off!"

But Bill says, "Hold on. Did you search him?"

"No. Didn't you?"

"No. So he's still got his share of the cash."

"Well, then, come along. No use to take this stuff and leave the money."

So they got out of the lifeboat and went back to the room where the man was tied up.

The door slammed. In half a second, I was in the boat, and Jim came after me. I cut the rope and away we went!

We didn't touch an oar, and we didn't whisper, nor hardly even breathe. We went gliding along, dead silent, past the tip of the stern. In a second or two, we was a hundred yards below the wreck, and the darkness soaked her up. We was safe and we knowed it.

Then Jim rowed the oars, and we took off after our raft. Now was the first time I begun to worry about the men. I begun to think how dreadful it was, even for murderers, to be in such a fix. So I says to Jim, "The first light we see, we'll land in a hiding place. Then I'll go and tell some kind of story, and get somebody to go get that gang off the boat."

But that idea failed. For pretty soon, it begun to storm again, this time worse than ever. After a long time, the rain let up, but the lightning keep up. By and by, a flash showed us a black thing ahead, floating. We went for it.

It was the raft, and we was mighty glad to get on it again. The skiff was half full of the stuff that gang had stolen. We loaded it onto the raft. I told Jim to float along down in the raft and keep a light burning till I come. Then I got back in the skiff and headed for the village. I seen a lantern on a ferryboat. I looked for the watchman and found him asleep on the deck. I come up and give him a shove and begun to cry.

The skiff was half full of the stuff that gang had stolen. We loaded it onto the raft. I told Jim to float along down in the raft and keep a light burning till I come.

He looked scared, but when he seen it was only me, he said, "What's up? Don't cry, son. What's the trouble?"

I says, "Pap and mam and sis and—"

Then I broke down. He says, "Oh dang it, now, don't cry. What's the matter with 'em?"

"They're in a heap of trouble. If you'd take your ferry-boat and go up there—"

"Up where? Where are they?"

"On the wreck."

"What wreck?"

"Why, there ain't but one."

"What, you don't mean the Walter Scott?"

"Yes."

"Good land! What are they doin' *there?*"

"Miss Hooker was visiting over in town. She started over in the horse-ferry with her servant, to stay all night at her friend's house. They lost their steering oar and swung around. They went floating down the river about two mile, then crashed into the wreck. The ferry man and horses and servant were lost but Miss Hooker got aboard. Well, after dark, we come along and didn't notice the wreck till we was right on it. So we hit it. We shouted, but nobody could hear. So Papa said somebody's got to get ashore and get help somehow. I was the only one that could swim, so I made a dash for it."

"Well, I'd like to help, but who's going to pay for it?"

"Miss Hooker, she told me that her Uncle Hornback—"

"Great guns! Is *he* her uncle? Look here, you walk down into the village to the tavern. Ask them to take you to Jim Hornback's. Tell him I'll have his niece all safe before he can get to town."

I headed for town until he turned the corner. Then I went back and got in my skiff. I went upshore and waited. I couldn't rest easy till I could see the ferryboat start. But I felt pretty good about myself for trying to save that gang. I wished the widow knowed about it. She would be proud of me for helping. After all, no-goods is the kind that good people takes the most interest in helping.

Well, before long, here comes the wreck, sliding along down! A kind of cold chill went through me. She was very deep. There weren't much chance for anybody being alive in her. I pulled all around her and yelled a little. There weren't any answer. I felt sad about the gang. Then here comes the ferryboat, so I moved on out of sight. When I looked back, I saw the ferry hang around the wreck looking for Miss Hooker's remainders. Pretty soon the ferry boat gave up, and I went booming down the river.

It did seem a long time before Jim's light showed up. By the time I got there, the sky was getting gray. We found an island, hid the raft, and sunk the skiff. Then we turned in and slept like dead people.

CHAPTER FOURTEEN

W hen we got up, we went through the stuff the gang had stolen off the shipwreck. We found boots, blankets, clothes, books, and all sorts of things. We hadn't ever been this rich before. We rested all afternoon. I told Jim what happened on the wreck and at the ferryboat. I said these kinds of things was adventures, but he said he didn't want no more adventures. I read to Jim about kings and dukes and such, about how they dressed and how much style they had. I read about how they called each other "your majesty" and "your grace" instead of mister.

"I didn't know there was so many of 'em," Jim said. "I ain't heard about none of 'em but old King Solomon, unless you count the kings in a pack of cards. How much do a king get?"

"Get?" I says. "Why, they can have as much as they want."

"And what they got to do, Huck?"

"*They* don't do nothing. They just set around. Except when there's war. Then they go to war. At other times, when things is dull, they fuss with the **parliament.**[1] But mostly they hang around with their wives. King Solomon had about a million wives."

"Yet they say Solomon the wisest man that ever live. I don't take no stock in that. Why would a wise man want to live in the midst of such a hubbub all the time?"

"Well, he *was* the wisest man, anyway, because the widow she told me so."

"I don't care what the widow say. He weren't no wise man. Do you know about that child that he was going to chop in two?"[2]

"Yes, the widow told me all about it."

"*Well,* then! You just take a look at it a minute. That stump is one woman. You're the other one. I'm Solomon. And this here dollar bill's the child. Both of you claims it. What do I do? Do I ask around

---

[1] **parliament**—body of decision-makers for the government in some European countries, similar to the Congress in the United States.

[2] Solomon, the King of Israel, is famous for his wisdom. To settle an argument about a child, he once suggested chopping the child into two parts and giving half of the child to each of the women claiming to be its mother.

and find out which one of you the bill belongs to? No, I whack the bill in two, and give half to you and half to the stump. That's the way Solomon was going to do with the child. Now I ask you, what's the use of half a bill? And what use is half a child?"

"But, Jim, you've missed the whole point."

"Don't talk to me about your points. I knows what I knows. And mind you, the real point lays in the way Solomon was raised. You take a man that's got only one or two children. Is that man going to waste his children? No, he ain't. He can't afford it. He knows how to value 'em. But you take a man that's got about five million children running around the house, and it's different. Take away a child or two and it don't matter to Solomon. There's plenty more."

I never did see such a man as Jim. If he got an idea in his head once, there weren't no getting it out again. He was the most down on Solomon of anyone I ever see. So I started talking about King Louis Sixteenth. He got his head cut off in France a long time ago. His little boy would've been king, but they shut him up in jail. Some say he died there.

"Poor little guy," says Jim.

"But some says he got away and came to America."

"There ain't no kings here, is there, Huck?"

"No."

"Then he can't get another job here. What's he going to do?"

"Well, I don't know. Some of them become police. Some of them teach people how to talk French."

"Why, Huck, don't the French people talk the same we does?"

"No, Jim. You couldn't understand a word they say. Suppose a man was to come to you and say **Polly-voo-franzy.**[3] What would you think?"

"I'd bust him over the head."

"Shucks, it's only saying do you know how to talk French."

"Well, then why don't he just say it?"

"Why, he is saying it."

"Well, it's a silly way to say it."

"Look, Jim, does a cat talk like we do?"

"No."

"Well, does a cow?"

"No."

[3] **Polly-voo-franzy**—Huck means, "Parlez-vous français?" or "Do you speak French?"

"Does a cat talk like a cow, or a cow talk like a cat?"

"No, they don't."

"And ain't it natural for a cat and a cow to talk different from us?"

"Sure it is."

"Well, then ain't it natural for a *Frenchman* to talk different from us?"

"Is a cat a man, Huck?"

"No."

Well, then, there ain't no sense in a cat talkin' like a man. Is a *Frenchman* a man?"

"Yes."

"Well, then. Why don't he *talk* like a man?"

I could see it weren't no use wasting words. I couldn't teach Jim to argue. So I quit.

CHAPTER FIFTEEN

We figured that in three more nights we would be in Cairo, where the Ohio River comes in. That was what we was after. We would sell the raft and get on a steamboat. We would go way up the Ohio River among the **Free States.**[1]

Well, the second night a fog rolled in. We looked for a tow-head to tie onto, but when I went ahead in the boat, I couldn't find anything but little **saplings.**[2] I passed the line around one of them, but the waves were so high, the raft come booming

---

[1] **Free States**—Slaves were free in some northern states at the time Twain set this story. If Jim could get to a Free State, his master would have no claim on him.

[2] **saplings**—small, young trees; Huck is looking for a sandbar with stronger trees in order to tie the boat securely.

down and tore the saplings out by the roots. I could see the fog closing down. It made me so scared I couldn't move. Then there weren't no raft in sight. I jumped into the boat and began to paddle, but it didn't move. I was in such a hurry I hadn't untied her. I got up and tried to untie her. My hands shook.

I took out after the raft. When I flew by the foot of it, I shot out into solid white fog. After that, I had no idea which way I was going. I set still and whooped and listened. Somewhere I heard a small whoop. I went tearing after it, listening to hear it again. The next time it came, I weren't heading for it but away to the right of it. And the next time, I was heading away to the left of it. Well, I fought along, and soon I hears the whoop *behind* me. I throwed the paddle down. I kept hearing the whoop in different places, and I kept answering till it was in front of me again. I knowed the current had swung the boat downstream and I was all right.

Nothing looks or sounds right in a fog. The trees on the bank looked like ghosts. I came up close to the bank, then the waves throwed me back again. Now it was white and still.

I just gave up then. I knowed what the matter was. That cut bank was an island, and Jim had gone down the other side of it. It might be five or six miles long. For about a half an hour, I whooped now and then. At last I heard the answer a long ways off. I tried to follow it, but I couldn't do it. You never knowed a sound could **dodge**[3] around so much. Well, I seemed to be in the open river again. I couldn't hear no whoop, so I lied down in the canoe. I didn't want to go to sleep, but I couldn't help it.

When I waked up, the stars was shining bright. The fog was all gone, and I was spinning down a big bend. I looked down stream and seen a black speck on the water. When I got to it, it was just some logs. Then I see another speck and chased that one, then another. This time, it was the raft.

"Is that you, Huck? And you ain't dead or drowned?"

When I got to it, Jim was setting there with his head down, asleep. One oar was broke off. The raft was covered with leaves and branches and dirt.

"Hello, Jim," I said. "Have I been asleep? Why didn't you wake me up?"

"Is that you, Huck? And you ain't dead or drowned? It's too good to be true, honey. Let me look at you, child. No, you ain't dead. You's back again, just the same old Huck, thanks to goodness!"

---

[3] **dodge**—to avoid or get away from.

"What's the matter with you, Jim? You been drinking?"

"Huck Finn, you look me in the eye. Ain't you been gone away?" Jim asked.

"Gone away? Where would I go to?"

"Well you answer me this. Didn't you go out in the boat to look for a tow-head?"

"What tow-head? I ain't seen no tow-head," I said to Jim.

"You ain't seen no tow-head? Looky here, didn't the line pull loose and the raft go hummin' down the river? Didn't I leave you behind in the fog?"

"What fog?" I asked, pretending nothing happened.

"Why, the fog that's been around all night," said Jim. "And didn't you whoop, and didn't I whoop, till we got mixed up? And didn't one of us got lost, and the other one was just as good as lost because he didn't know where he was? And didn't I crash on them islands and almost get drowned?"

"Well, this is too much for me, Jim. I ain't seen no fog, nor no islands, nor no troubles. I been setting here talking with you all night till you went to sleep, and then I done the same. You must've been dreaming."

"Now how is I going to dream all that in ten minutes?" Jim asked.

"Well, you did dream it, because it didn't happen."

"Well, dog my cats if it ain't the most real dream I ever see."

"Tell me all about it, Jim."

So Jim told me the whole thing, just as it happened. He did paint it up some. Then he said he must explain it. He said the first tow-head stood for a man that would try to do us some good. The big wave stood for another man that would get us away from him. The whoops was warnings that would come to us now and then. The tow-heads was troubles we would get into. But we would make it to the big clear river, which was the Free States. Then we wouldn't have no more trouble.

"Well, Jim," I says, "then what does these things stand for?" It was the leaves and trash on the raft and the smashed oar. You could see them now that the sky had cleared.

Jim looked at the trash, and then he looked at me. He looked at me steady, without smiling. "What do they stand for? I'll to tell you. My heart was almost broke because you was lost. I didn't care no more what became of me and the raft. And when I wake up and find you back again, the tears come. I was so thankful, I could've got down on my knees and kissed your foot.

And all you was thinking about was how you could make a fool of old Jim with a lie. Them leaves and dirt is *trash*, and trash is what people is that puts dirt on the head of their friends and makes 'em ashamed."

"My heart was almost broke because you was lost. "

Then he got up slow and walked to the wigwam. He went in there without saying anything but that. But that was enough. It made me feel so mean, I could've kissed *his* foot to get him to take it back. I didn't do him no more mean tricks. I wouldn't have done that one if I'd known it would make him feel that way.

CHAPTER SIXTEEN

We slept most all day, and started out at dark. The night clouded up and got hot. We talked about Cairo, and wondered whether we would know it when we got to it. Jim said the two big rivers joined together there. But I said we might think we were passing the foot of an island and coming into the same old river again. That upset Jim—and me too. So the question was, what to do?

I said I'd go ashore the first time a light showed. I'd tell them Pap was behind and wanted to know how far it was to Cairo. Jim thought it was a good idea, so we looked out for a town. He said he'd be sure to see it, because he'd be a free man[1] at that minute. But if he missed it, he'd be in slave country again, with no more chance for freedom.

---

[1] Cairo is in Illinois, which was a Free State for slaves. By reaching Cairo, Jim would become a free man.

I begun to get it through my head that he was almost free—and who was to blame for it? Why, *me*. I was to blame. I couldn't get that off my mind. I tried to act like I weren't to blame, but it weren't no use. I knowed he was a runaway. I could've gone ashore and told somebody. I couldn't get around that.

I got to feeling so bad, I almost wished I was dead. I paced up and down the raft. Jim paced up and down past me. Neither of us could keep still. Jim talked out loud all the time while I was talking to myself. He was telling the first thing he would do when he got to a Free State. He would save up every cent till he earned enough to buy his wife. She lived on a farm close to where Miss Watson lived. Then they would both work to buy the two children. If their children's master wouldn't sell the children, they'd get an **Abolitionist**[2] to go and steal them.

It almost froze me to hear such talk. Jim wouldn't ever dare to talk that way till he was almost free. Here was this slave who I helped to run away, saying he would steal his children—children that belonged to a man who had done me no harm.

---

[2] **Abolitionist**—person who tried to help free the slaves when the U.S. still practiced slavery.

At last I says to myself, "It ain't too late yet. I'll go ashore at the first light and tell."

Just then, Jim says, "We're safe, Huck, we're safe! That's good old Cairo, I just know it!"

"I'll go see, Jim," I says. "It might not be, you know."

> " Jim won't ever forget you, Huck. You're the best friend Jim's ever had. And you're the only friend old Jim's got now."

"Pretty soon I'll be shoutin' for joy. I'm a free man, thanks to Huck. Jim won't ever forget you, Huck. You're the best friend Jim's ever had. And you're the only friend old Jim's got now."

I was already paddling off, ready to turn him in. When he says this, it took everything out of me. I went along slow, then, and Jim called out, "There you go, the old true Huck, the only white man that ever kept his promise to old Jim."

Well, I just felt sick. But I says, I *got* to do it. Right then, along comes a skiff with two men on it. They had guns. One of them says, "What's that, over there?"

"A raft," I says.

"Do you belong on it?"

"Yes, sir?"

"Any men on it?"

"Only one, sir."

"Well, five slaves ran off tonight. Is your man white or black?"

I didn't answer. I tried to, but the words wouldn't come. So I just give up trying and says, "He's white."

"We better go and see for ourselves."

"I wish you would," says I, "because it's Pap that's there, and he's sick. So is **mam**[3] and Mary Ann."

"We're in a hurry, boy, but we'll help."

"Pap will be mighty happy. Everybody goes away when I want them to help me."

"Well, that's mean. Odd, too. Say, boy, what's wrong with your father?"

"It's the–a–the–well, it ain't anything, much."

They stopped pulling. One says, "Boy, that's a lie. What is wrong with your Pap?"

"Don't leave us, please."

"Your Pap's got the **smallpox**[4] and you know it. Why didn't you say so? Do you want to spread it all over?"

"Well," says I, "I've told everybody before. Then they just go away and leave us."

---

[3] **mam**—slang for mom.

[4] **smallpox**—an often deadly disease that leaves ugly scars and spreads from person to person very easily.

"Poor kid. We feel sorry for you, but we don't want the smallpox. So you go down about twenty miles, and you'll come to a town. Here, I'll put a twenty-dollar gold piece on this board, and you get it when it floats by. I feel mean to leave you, but we can't fool with smallpox, don't you see?"

"Hold on," says the other man, "here's a twenty from me. Good-bye, boy. If you see any runaway slaves, nab them, and you can make some more money."

"Good-bye, sir," says I. "I won't let no runaways get by me if I can help it."

They went off, and I got aboard the raft, feeling bad, because I could see it weren't no use for me to try to do right. A body that don't get started right when he's little ain't got no hope. Then I says to myself, suppose you would've given Jim up. Would you feel better than what you do now? No, says I. I'd feel just as bad as I do now. Well, then, says I, what's the use in doing right when the results is about the same? I couldn't answer that. So I reckoned I would do whichever come in handy at the time.

When I got to the raft, Jim was in the river, with just his nose sticking out. He says, "I was listening to all the talk. I hid in the river in case they come aboard. But my, how you did fool them, Huck! You saved old Jim. Old Jim ain't going to forget you for that."

Then we talked about the money. Jim said we could go by steamboat now. He said the money would take us as far as we wanted to go in the Free States. The next night at about ten, we saw the lights of a town. I went off to ask about it. Pretty soon I found a man in a fishing boat.

"Mister, is that town Cairo?" I asked.

"Cairo? No."

"What town is it, mister?"

"If you want to know, go and find out."

I went back to the raft. Jim was awful sad. We passed another town before daylight, but it wasn't Cairo neither. I says, "Maybe we went by Cairo in the fog that night."

"Don't talk about it, Huck. I can't have no good luck. I always knew that rattlesnake skin weren't through with its work."

We talked over what to do. We'd have to head back the other way. We slept all day back in the trees. Then when we went back to the raft, the canoe was gone!

So we shoved out, after dark, on the raft.

You can buy canoes off of rafts laying along the shore. We hoped to buy one, but we didn't see any rafts for three hours. It got to be very late and still.

Then along comes a steamboat up the river. We could hear her coming through the fog, but we didn't see her until she was too close. She aimed right for us. She looked like a black cloud with rows of glow worms around it. The guards yelled at us. There was a ringing of bells and a whistling of steam. Jim jumped off on one side and I jumped off the other, just as she crashed through the raft.

> **Jim jumped off on one side and I jumped off the other, just as she crashed through the raft.**

I dived for the bottom. I knew a thirty-foot wheel had to go over me. I wanted to give it plenty of room. I stayed under water a minute and a half. Then I bounced to the top in a hurry, nearly busting. That boat was already up the river, out of sight in the thick fog.

I called out for Jim lots of times, but he didn't answer. Finally, I grabbed a log and paddled to shore, pushing it ahead of me. I climbed up the bank. I went looking around and came to a big, log house. I was going to rush by, but a lot of dogs jumped out and started barking at me. I knew better than to move an inch.

CHAPTER SEVENTEEN

Somebody spoke out of a window. "Who's there?"

I says, "It's me."

"Who's me?"

"George Jackson, sir."

"What do you want?"

" I only want to go by, sir, but your dogs won't let me."

"What are you doing around here this time of night?"

"I fell off the steamboat."

"Look here, if you're telling the truth, don't be afraid. Nobody will hurt you. Stand right where you are. Is there anybody with you?"

"No, sir."

I heard the people stirring in the house. They put the light behind the front door and took their places. The man called out, "Now, George Jackson, do you know the Shepherdsons?"

"No, sir, I never heard of them."

"Well, that may be so, and it may not. Step forward slow. If there's anybody with you, let him keep back or he'll be shot. Push the door open slowly, you hear?"

I couldn't have hurried if I'd wanted to. The dogs followed me. I put my hand on the door and pushed it a little. Somebody said, "Put your head in." I done it, but I thought they would take it off.

The candle was on the floor, and there they all was, looking at me. Three big men pointed guns at me. The oldest was about sixty, the other two were thirty or more, and all were good-looking. I also saw the sweetest old gray-headed lady and two young women. The old man says, "Come in."

As soon as I was in, he locked the door. They all went into a big **parlor**[1] and looked at me and said, "Why he ain't a Shepherdson." Then the old man searched me, just to make sure. The old lady sent a servant to get me something to eat.

She says to the youngest son, "Buck, take this little stranger and get him some of your dry clothes."

---

[1] **parlor**—room used for entertaining.

Buck looked about as old as me—thirteen or fourteen. He says, "Ain't there no Shepherdsons around?"

They said, no, it was a false alarm.

"Well, he says, "if there'd been some, I would've got one."

They all laughed. When we got to his room, he gave me a shirt and some pants. I put them on. He started telling me about a blue jay and a rabbit he had catched in the woods. Then he asked me where Moses was when the candle went out. I said I didn't know.

"Well, guess," he says.

"How am I going to guess," says I, "when I never heard about it before?"

"But you can guess, can't you?"

"I don't know where he was," says I. "Where was he?"

"Why, he was in the dark! That's where he was!"

"Well, if you knowed where he was, what did you ask me for?"

"Why, it's a riddle, don't you see? How long are you going to stay here? You got to stay always. We can have some great times." He kept talking as we went downstairs to the table.

Cold corn-pone, cold beef, butter and butter-milk—that is what they had for me down there. There ain't nothing better. They all asked me questions, and I told them that my family just died and I took our things on a riverboat, but I fell off. So they said I could have a home there as long as I wanted it.

It was a nice family and a nice house too, with a real brass doorknob and a big fireplace. The clock over the fireplace had a **pendulum**[2] and a picture of a town painted on the glass. They had pictures hung on the walls. One of the daughters, who was dead, had made them when she was only fifteen years old. One showed a woman at a grave. Another one was a young lady crying and holding a dead bird. In another picture, a lady looked out a window at the moon, crying. She held an open letter and a **locket**.[3] Young Emmeline died before she finished the last one. Now they kept the picture over the bed in her room. Every time her birthday come they hung flowers on it.

---

[2] **pendulum**—the swinging hand below a grandfather clock that tick-tocks.
[3] **locket**—necklace with space for a picture inside.

This young girl also kept a **scrapbook**[4] when she was alive. She would paste **obituaries**[5] in it. Then she would write poems from her own head. Buck said she could write anything you choose, as long as it was sad. Every time someone died, she would write a poem before the dead body was cold. The neighbors said it was the doctor first, then Emmeline, then the **undertaker.**[6] She did not live long, poor thing.

I liked that family, dead ones and all. I didn't want anything to come between us.

---

[4] **scrapbook**—book used to keep pictures, clippings, or other memories.

[5] **obituaries**—short articles about people who have recently died.

[6] **undertaker**—person who prepares bodies for burial.

CHAPTER EIGHTEEN

Colonel Grangerford was a gentleman, you see. So was his family. He was very tall and very slim. He was clean-shaved every morning. He had thin lips and black eyes. His hair hung to his shoulders. Every day of his life he put on a clean shirt and a white suit. He weren't ever loud. He was as kind as he could be. Everybody was always good mannered where he was. Everybody loved to have him around, too.

When him and the old lady came down in the morning, all the family got up out of their chairs. Then Tom and Bob handed him a drink. He bowed and said thank you. Then we all drank to the old people.

Bob was the oldest, and Tom next. They dressed well and wore broad hats. Then there was Miss Charlotte. She was twenty-five, and nice looking.

So was her sister, Miss Sophia, but she was only twenty. Each person had their own servant to wait on them. Mine had an easy time, because I weren't used to having anybody do anything for me. This was all there was of the family, now, but there used to be more. Three sons got killed and Emmeline died.

The old man owned a lot of farms and more than a hundred slaves. Sometimes people would come from miles around. They would stay for days and have dances, picnics, and parties. These people was mostly **kinfolks**[1] of the family. The men brought their guns with them.

There was another clan of **aristocracy**[2] around there named Shepherdson. They was just as rich as the Grangerfords. The two families used the same steamboat landing. Sometimes when I went up there, I saw them on their fine horses.

One day Buck and me was in the woods and heard a horse coming. Buck says, "Quick! Hide in the trees!"

Pretty soon a young man comes down the road. It was young Harney Shepherdson. I heard Buck's gun go off, and Harney's hat fell off. He grabbed his gun and rode to where we was hid. But we

---

[1] **kinfolks**—extended family members such as aunts, uncles and cousins.

[2] **aristocracy**—the rich class.

didn't wait. We never stopped running till we got home. Soon as I could get Buck alone, I says, "Did you want to kill him, Buck?"

"You bet I did."

"What did he do to you?"

"Nothing."

"Well, then, what did you want to kill him for?"

"Because of the feud."

"What's a feud?"

"A man has a quarrel with another man, and kills him. Then that other man's brother kills him. Then the other brothers on both sides goes after one another. Pretty soon everybody's killed off, and there ain't no more feud. But it takes a long time."

"Has this one been going on long, Buck?"

"Well, it started thirty years ago."

"What was the trouble about, Buck? Land?"

"How do I know? It was so long ago."

"Has there been many killed, Buck?"

"Yes, but they don't always kills a fella. Pa's got a few buck-shot in him. He don't mind it cause he don't weigh much anyway. Bob's been carved up some and Tom's been hurt once or twice."

"Has anybody been killed this year, Buck?"

> *"Well, then, what did you want to kill him for?" "Because of the feud."*

"Yes, we got one and they got one." Then he went on to tell the story of old Baldy Shepherdson shooting his cousin Bud from behind.

"I think that old man was a coward, Buck."

"No, there ain't a coward amongst the Shepherdsons. And there ain't no cowards amongst the Grangerfords, either."

Next Sunday we all went to church on horseback. The men took their guns along. The Shepherdsons done the same. It was pretty ornery[3] preaching, all about brotherly love. But everybody said it was a good sermon.[4] They all talked it over going home.

After dinner I went up to our room and thought I would take a nap. Miss Sophia stopped me. She asked if I would do something for her and not tell anybody. I said I would. Then she said she'd left her Testament[5] on the seat at church. She asked me to go get it for her. So I went up the road. There was nobody at the church but a hog or two. The hogs like to go inside where it's cool.

---

[3] **ornery**—unpleasant.

[4] **sermon**—speech or preaching done by a minister.

[5] **Testament**—New Testament, the part of the Bible that tells the story of Jesus Christ.

I picked up the book and out drops a paper with "Half-past two" wrote on it. When I got home, Miss Sophia was waiting for me. She pulled me into her room and shut the door. Then she looked in the Bible till she found the paper. As soon as she read it she looked happy. She hugged me and said I was the best boy in the world, and asked me not to tell anybody.

I went down to the river to think. Pretty soon I saw my servant walking along behind. He says, "Mr. George, if you'll come down to the swamp, I'll show you a stack of **water moccasins.**"[6]

So I says, "All right. Go ahead."

I followed him a half mile. Then we waded out in the water a long ways. We came to a little flat piece of land, thick with trees and bushes.

"Go in there," he says. "That's where they is." Then he went away.

I went into the place and found a big open patch. A man lay sleeping there. It was my old Jim! I waked him up. He nearly cried, he was so glad to see me again. He said he'd swam along behind me that night and heard me yell. He didn't shout back, because he didn't want anybody to pick him up and make him a slave again.

---

[6] **water moccasins**—members of a species of harmless water snakes.

"I got hurt and couldn't swim fast," he says. "When you landed, I tried to catch up, but then I saw that house, so I stayed in the woods for a day. Some of the servants come along on their way to the fields. They showed me this place, where the dogs can't track me because of the water. And they bring me food every night and tells me how you're doing."

"Why didn't you tell them to bring me here sooner?"

"Well, there weren't no use until we could do something. I been buying pots and pans and food. I been fixing the raft at night."

"*What* raft, Jim?"

"Our old raft."

"You mean to say it weren't smashed up?"

"Not bad. Now she's all fixed up again. We got a new lot of stuff, too. We're ready to go."

I don't want to talk much about the next day. I waked up about dawn and thought about how still it was. Next I noticed that Buck was up and gone. So was everybody else. I found Jack and asked, "What's happening?"

Says he, "Don't you know, Master George? Miss Sophia's run off! She run off in the night to marry Harney Shepherdson. The family found it out about half an hour ago, and there weren't no time lost. The women went to tell the other kinfolks. Old Master Saul and the boys took the guns and rode up the river. They want to catch that young man before he can cross the river with Miss Sophia.

I ran up the river road as fast as I could. I begin to hear guns a good ways off. When I come to the log store, I climbed a tree and watched. Four or five men on horses were yelling at two boys behind the wood stack. The two boys sat back to back behind the wood, shooting at the men.

By and by the men turned away. Then one of the boys stood up and shot one of them. All the men grabbed the hurt one and carried him into the store. The two boys ran to the woodpile in front of my tree. One of the boys was Buck. The men rode away. As soon as they left, I called out to Buck. He was awful surprised. He told me to let him know when the men come into sight again. Then Buck began to cry. He said his father and his two brothers was killed, and two or three of the enemy. The Shepherdsons had been waiting for them when they got there. I asked him about Harney and Miss Sophia. He said they got across the river. I was glad, but Buck said he wish he'd killed Harney that day we shot at him.

All of a sudden, bang! bang! bang! go the guns. The men had come through the woods from behind without their horses! The boys jumped into the river, both of them hurt. As they swam, the men ran along the bank, shouting out, "Kill them, kill them!" It made me so sick, I almost fell out of the tree. I ain't going to tell *all* that happened. I wished I hadn't ever come ashore that night, to see such things. I ain't ever going to get free of them. Lots of times I dream about them.

All of a sudden, bang! bang! bang! go the guns. The men had come through the woods from behind without their horses! The boys jumped into the river, both of them hurt.

I stayed in the tree till dark, afraid to come down. Sometimes I heard guns off in the woods. I was too upset to ever go near that house again. I thought I was to blame, somehow. That piece of paper meant that Miss Sophia was to meet Harney at half past two. I should have told her father. Then maybe he would've locked her up, and this awful mess wouldn't have happened.

When I got down out of the tree, I crept along the river. I found the two bodies laying in the water. I pulled them ashore and covered their faces. I cried when I covered up Buck's face, for he was good to me.

I went to the swamp. When I found Jim and the raft, he hugged me. He says, "Bless you, child, I was sure you was dead again."

"All right, that's good," I says, "they'll think I've been killed and floated down the river. Don't lose no time, Jim. Head for the big water as fast as you can."

I never felt safe till the raft was two miles below there. Then we figured we was free. We said there weren't no home like a raft, after all.

CHAPTER NINETEEN

Two or three days and nights went by. We traveled by night and hid in the day. Just before daybreak, we'd tie up the raft. Then we'd cut up young branches and lay them over, to hide it. We'd set out the fishing lines. Next, we'd swim the river to freshen up. Then we'd watch the daylight come and listen to the bullfrogs. First the woods on the other side would take shape, then you'd see white in the sky. A breeze would float across the river, smelling of woods and flowers. Then the songbirds would go at it. Next you've got the full day, and everything smiling in the sun.

After breakfast we would sleep. A steamboat coughing up steam would wake us sometimes. Then for an hour there wouldn't be a sound. Once there was a thick fog and a raft went by so close we could hear them talking, but we couldn't see them. It made you feel scared. Jim said he believed it was spirits, but I says, "No, spirits wouldn't say, 'darn the darn fog'."

Soon as it was night, we shoved out into the river again. We let her float and put our legs in the water. Sometimes we could hear a **fiddle**[1] or a song coming from one of the rafts. We had the sky, up there, all speckled with stars. We would lie on our backs and look at them and wonder if they was made or only just happened. Jim thought they was made, but I thought they only just happened. I said it would have took too long to *make* so many. Jim said the moon could've *laid* them like eggs. Well, that sounded all right, because I've see a frog lay almost as many. When we watched the stars that fell, Jim says they were spoiled and got tossed out of the nest. When the first spark showed in a window again, it meant morning was coming, so we hunted a place to tie up and hide.

One morning, I found a canoe. I got in and went down a creek, to see if I could get some berries. When I passed a cow path that crossed the creek, here comes two men, running as fast as they could. They called out and begged me to save their lives.

---

[1] **fiddle**—a musical instrument; violin.

They said that men and dogs were chasing them. As soon as they got in, I took off.

One of these fellows was about seventy. He had a bald head and a gray beard. He had old blue jeans stuffed into his boot tops. He had a long-tailed coat. Both of them had big ratty-looking **carpet bags**[2] The other man was about thirty and dressed about as strangely. After breakfast we sat and talked. Then I could see that these two fellas didn't know each other.

"What got you into trouble?" says the bald one to the other one.

"Well, I'd been selling a paste that cleans the teeth. It takes off most of the tooth too. I stayed about one night too long. What's your story?"

"Well, I'd been running a **temperance**[3] **revival**[4] for about a week. I was making lots of money, till they found me with a jug. So a slave woke me up this morning and told me the people was coming with their dogs and horses. They planned to tar

---

[2] **carpet bag**—a traveling bag made of carpet; after the Civil War, Northerners who went to the South to sell things for profit were known as "carpet baggers."

[3] **temperance**—not drinking any alcohol or the movement to end the drinking of alcohol.

[4] **revival**—special meeting to stir interest in religion or to help a cause such as the temperance movement.

and feather[5] me. Well, I didn't wait around for breakfast. I took off."

"Old man," says the young one, "Let's team up together. What do you think?"

"I'll think about it. What's your line of work?"

"Printer, by trade. And I'm an actor. I take a turn at **hypnotism**[6] when there's a chance. I teach singing and reading maps. Oh, I do most anything, as long as it ain't work. What's your line?"

"I've done some doctoring in my time. Laying on of hands[7] is my best hook. And I can tell a fortune pretty good, when I've got somebody to find out the facts for me."

No one said anything for awhile, then the younger man, "Alas!"

"What're you alassin' about?" says the baldhead.

"To think I should have to be with lowly people like these." He began to wipe his eyes.

"Ain't we good enough for you?" says the bald man. So the young man carried on and cried and finally told the source of his pain.

"Ah, you would not believe the secret of my birth. By rights, I am a duke!"

---

[5] tar and feather—to punish a person by smearing them with tar and then covering them with feathers.

[6] **hypnotism**—the act of controlling someone's will.

[7] laying on of hands—healing someone by blessing them or saying a prayer over them.

Jim's eyes bugged out when he heard that. Mine did too. Then the bald one says, "No! You can't mean it!"

"Yes. My great-grandfather was the oldest son of the Duke of Bridgewater. He came to this country about the end of the last century. He married and died, leaving a son. When his own father died, his younger brother said he was king. The real duke was just a baby. I am related to that baby. And here I am, torn from my throne, hunted by men, and left to live with thieves on a raft!"

Jim pitied him ever so much, and so did I. We tried to help him. He said it would make him feel better if we waited on him at mealtime and bowed when we spoke to him. He asked us to call him "your grace" or "your lordship." He would also let us call him "Bridgewater."

Well, that was all easy, so we done it. But the old man got quiet. He seemed to have something on his mind. So along in the afternoon, he spoke up.

"Look here, Bilgewater, I'm sorry for you. But you ain't the only person with a secret of his birth." Then *he* begins to cry.

"What do you mean?"

"Bilgewater, can I trust you?" says the old man, sobbing.

"To the bitter death!" He took the old man by the hand and says, "Tell me the secret of your being."

"Bilgewater, I am the poor lost son of Louie the Sixteenth."

"You are? Then you must be six or seven hundred years old!"

"Yes, but trouble has brought these gray hairs and balditude.[8] Gentleman, you see before you the real King of France."

It didn't take me long to make up my mind that these liars weren't kings nor dukes but just low-down cheats.

Well, he cried so much that me and Jim didn't know what to do. So we did what we'd done before with the duke. He said it made him feel better if people got down on one knee to speak to him. We must always called him "your majesty," and wait on him first at meals. The duke didn't look happy with the ways things was going, but the king acted friendly to him. He said his father thought a lot of the dukes of Bilgewater.

It didn't take me long to make up my mind that these liars weren't kings nor dukes but just low-down cheats. But I didn't let on. If I never learned

---

[8] balditude—Twain's slang or informal word for baldness.

nothing else from Pap, I learned that the best way to get along with his kind of people is to let them have their own way.

CHAPTER TWENTY

They asked us lots of questions. They wanted to know why we covered up the raft and hid out during the day. Was Jim a runaway slave? I asked, "Would a runaway slave run *south?*"

I had to explain things, so I said my pa and I came to live with my Uncle Ben. We brought Jim because he was all the family owned. We took a raft, but it got hit by a steamboat, and my pa drowned. People tried to take Jim away from me, so now we hide in the daytime and only go out at night.

The duke says, "I'll think of a plan so we can run the raft in the daytime if we want to."

Towards night it darkened up and looked like rain. The lightning shot across in the sky. The leaves shivered. So the duke and the king went into our wigwam to see the beds. Mine was made of straw, but Jim's was made of corn husks. There's always cobs in a corn-husk bed, and they poke into you and hurt. The duke wanted my bed, but the king say that he should have the straw bed. The duke made a fuss, but let him have it.

About ten o'clock it started to rain and blow hard. The king told us to both stay on watch. Then him and the duke went into the wigwam to sleep. How the wind did scream along! The lightning glared. The trees thrashed around. The thunder grumbled. The waves came up high. I felt sleepy, so Jim said he would take the first part of my watch. The wigwam was full, so I laid outside. I didn't mind the rain because it was warm. About two o'clock, the waves got higher. All of a sudden, along came a big one and washed me off the boat. It almost killed Jim laughing.

The next morning, the king and the duke started to plan. The duke got into his carpet bag and got a lot of printed flyers. In one **hand bill**,[1] he was a famous Shakespearean play actor named Garrick the Younger. In other bills he had a lot of other names, but he liked acting the most.

---

[1] **hand bill**—paper flyer announcing a show or sale.

"The first good town we come to, we'll rent a hall and put on a play," he says. How does that sound?"

"I'm in," says the king, "but I was too small to remember when Pap held plays at the palace. Can you learn me how to act?"

So the duke told him all about Romeo and Juliet. He said he was used to being Romeo, so the king could be Juliet.

"But if Juliet's such a young gal, Duke, my peeled head and my white beard is going to look bad on her, maybe."

"Don't you worry. These country folks won't ever think of that. Besides, you'll be in a costume, and that makes it all right."

He got out a long white cotton nightshirt and hat. The king was satisfied. The duke read the parts, prancing around to show how it had to be done. Then he gave the book to the king. He told him to learn his part by heart.

There was a little town around the bed. After dinner the duke said he knew how to run the raft in daylight. He and the king would go to town and fix it so we could. I went along in the boat because we were out of coffee.

When we got to town, there weren't nobody stirring. We found a sick slave lying in a back yard. He said everybody was gone to a church camp meeting back in the woods. The king said he'd go work the camp meeting. The duke said he would look for a printing office. He found one standing empty with no doors locked. The printers had all gone to the meeting. The duke took off his coat and said he was all right, now. So me and the king went off to the meeting.

The woods was full of horses and wagons. Folks had come from miles around. They sold lemonade in sheds. The preaching went on under bigger sheds. People sat on logs, but the preachers stood on stages. The first preacher we come to would sing out a line, then the people would sing it. He called people to come up and get clean of their sins. He said he would heal their sickness and help them find the doors of heaven. And so on. Folks worked their way up to the front, where they sang, shouted, and threw themselves down on the straw.

Well, pretty soon the king got going. You could hear him over everybody. Next he went up on to the stage. The preacher told him to speak, and he done it. He said he was a pirate in the Indian Ocean for thirty years. He'd been robbed last night, but he was glad to be here. He was happy for the first time in his life. Now he was going to work his way back to the Indian Ocean and turn all the pirates onto the true path. It would take him a long time to get there without any money, but he would get there. Every time he taught a pirate, he would say, "Don't thank me. Thank the dear people in Pokeville camp meeting. Thank that dear preacher, the best friend a pirate ever had."

And then he busted into tears, and so did everybody. Then somebody says, "Take up some money for him!"

So the king went all through the crowd with his hat, thanking the people who put money in it. The girls all kissed him, and everybody wanted him to stay at their houses. He said he was in too much of a hurry to get back to the Indian Ocean, to work on the pirates.

When we got back to the raft, he counted up eighty-seven dollars and seventy-five cents. He had also found a jug of whisky under a wagon. He said it was his best camp meeting yet.

The duke thought he'd done pretty well until the king showed up. He had printed two hand bills for farmers selling horses. He also sold ads for the paper. He took in nine dollars and a half. Then he showed us another little handbill he'd printed for us. It was a picture of a runaway slave with "$200 reward" under it. The picture looked just like Jim. It said he'd run away forty miles below New Orleans. Whoever would catch him and send him back could have the reward and expenses.

It was a picture of a runaway slave with "$200 reward" under it. The picture looked just like Jim.

"Now we can run in the daytime," says the duke. "Whenever we see anybody coming, we can tie Jim up with a rope, show this handbill, and say we caught him."

We all said the duke was pretty smart. We could start after we got far enough away from this town.

Late that night, Jim says, "Huck, does you think we're going to run across any more kings on this trip?"

"No," I says.

"Well," says he, "that's all right, then. I don't mind one or two kings, but that's enough."

CHAPTER TWENTY-ONE

The sun came up, but we went right on and didn't tie up the boat. After breakfast, the king tried to learn Romeo and Juliet. The duke told him not to shout "Romeo!" like a bull but to say it soft and sweet, like a young girl would do.

Well, next they practiced the sword fight. But by and by, the king tripped and fell off the raft. After that, they took a rest. The duke says, "Well, we'll want to make this a first-class show. I guess we'll add a little more to it. You can do the speech by Hamlet."[1]

The duke said the speech, and the old man liked it. He practiced until he got so he could do it well. The first chance we got, the duke had some hand bills printed.

---

[1] Hamlet—main character in one of Shakespeare's most famous plays.

One morning we saw a little town. We tied the boat at the mouth of a creek. All of us but Jim took the small boat and went down to find a place for our show. We got lucky. There was a circus in town. All the people came in from the country, on wagons and on horses. The circus would leave before night, so our show would have a good chance. The duke rented the court house for the play. Then we went around and hung our bills. The bills said it was for one night only. Adults would pay 25 cents. Children and servants could get in for 10 cents.

The nearer it got to noon, the thicker was the wagons and horses in the streets. Families brought their dinners and ate them in the wagons. By and by, the town drunk came along. His name was Boggs. He yelled at everyone till he nearly fell out of his saddle. He had a very red face. Everybody laughed at him. He said he had come to town to kill old Colonel Sherburn. He saw me and asked, "You ready to die?" Then he rode on. I was scared, but a man told me he didn't mean nothing. He never hurt anybody, even drunk.

Boggs rode to the biggest store in town. He called, "Come out here, Sherburn! You're the dog I'm after." He went on calling Sherburn names. The whole street filled up with people, listening and laughing. Then a proud man stepped out of the store. The crowd dropped back. He says, "I'm tired of this. I'll only take it till one o'clock. If you say anything about me after that, I'll come and find you."

Then he went inside. Everybody told Boggs to quit and go home. Boggs would not listen. He came back and kept it up. He shouted and threw his hat down in the mud. He rode around with his gray hair flying. In a few minutes, he came back with two friends. Somebody called his name. It was Colonel Sherburn, standing in the street with his gun pointed at the sky. Boggs turned to see who'd called him. The two friends ran off. Boggs said, "Don't shoot!" Then *bang!* goes the first shot. *Bang!* goes the second one. And Boggs fell backwards onto the ground.

Colonel Sherburn tossed his gun down and walked off. The crowd carried Boggs into a drug store. They laid him down and he made about a dozen long gasps. After that, he lay still. He was dead. His daughter had come, and she was screaming and crying. They had to pull her away from him.

Well, pretty soon the whole town came to see him. Then somebody said Sherburn should be hanged. Everybody agreed. They went away mad. The grabbed every **clothesline**[2] they could find to do the hanging.

---

[2] **clothesline**—cord strung between two poles; wet clothes are fastened to the line to dry.

CHAPTER TWENTY-TWO

The crowd ran up the street to Sherburn's house, yelling. Women and children watched from windows and trees. The crowd jammed into his little yard. "Tear down the fence!" they shouted. Just then, Sherburn stepped out onto his porch roof, once again holding his gun. He stood calmly as the crowd stepped back. He ran his eye slowly along the crowd. Then he laughed a mean laugh. He called them cowards and said they could never hang a man. He told them they were all just going along with the crowd. He said the only way they could hang people is in the dark, wearing masks. Then he told them to go home. The crowd soon broke up.

I didn't want to stay. I went to the circus and hung around behind the tent. Then I sneaked in under the tent. It was a really first-rate circus. First they all came riding in, two and two, a gentleman and a lady. The men wore their underwear. Every lady dressed like a queen. I never seen anything so lovely. They danced around on their horses. The ringmaster cracked his whip. The clown made jokes. All during the circus they done the most amazing things.

A drunken man came into the ring and wanted to ride one of the horses. The ringmaster tried to keep him out. The people yelled at the drunk, and that made him mad. He stomped around the ring. Some men came down to throw him out, but the ringmaster finally let him ride. Everyone laughed when the drunk got on the horse. The minute he did, the horse began to jump and buck. The rider's heels flew in the air. Two circus men tried to hold the horse, but they couldn't. They gave up, and the horse went tearing around the ring. People laughed and shouted. At last, the rider got into the saddle. The next minute, he stood up on the horse as it ran around the ring. He just stood there, sailing around as if he were never drunk. Then he began to pull off his clothes. All together, he took off 17 suits. There he was, slim and good looking in his costume. He skipped off the horse, bowed, and danced off to the dressing room. Everyone howled with pleasure. The ringmaster felt sick, I reckon. He was fooled by one of his own men.

That night we had our show. Only twelve people came. They laughed all the time, which made the duke mad. Everybody left before the show was over, all but one boy who was asleep. The duke said these Arkansaw types weren't ready for Shakespeare. They wanted low comedy, he decided. The next morning he made a new sign. It announced a play called *The King's Camelopard* or *The Royal Nonesuch!!!* It would show for three nights only. Tickets were twice as much as before. No ladies or children could come.

"If that doesn't bring them in," he said, "I don't know Arkansaw!"

CHAPTER TWENTY-THREE

All day the king and the duke set up the stage. They put up a curtain and a row of candles for footlights. That night, the house was full of men. When the place couldn't hold no more, the duke quit tending the door. He went around back and came onto the stage. He made a little speech. After he got everybody's hopes up, he rolled up the curtain. The king came prancing in on all fours, naked. He was painted all over with stripes, in all sorts of colors. The people went wild with laughter. When the king got done, he left the stage. They clapped till he came back and did it all again. Then they made him do it one more time.

Then the duke let the curtain down. He bowed to the people and said the great play will only show for two more nights.

"What? It's over?" twenty people called out. Then everybody got up mad and went on stage to beat up the the king and duke. A big man jumped up on a bench and shouted, "Hold on! We were tricked. But we don't want the whole town laughing at us. Let's go home and talk this show up. That way, we can fool the rest of the town."

"The judge is right," everybody says.

"All right, then. Go along home, and tell everybody to come and see the play."

Next night the house was jammed again. We fooled the crowd the same way. After supper, we hid the raft down the river a ways. The third night the house was packed again. But there were no new people, just people who came the first two nights. I could see that every man had something to throw in his pocket. I smelled rotten eggs and cabbages and things. When the place could hold no more, the duke gave a man a quarter to tend the door. Then he acted like he would head for the stage door. Instead he turned to me in the dark and said, "Walk fast, till we get away from the houses. Then run for the raft."

I done it. He done the same. We got to the raft, and in less than two seconds we were floating down stream, nobody talking. I thought the king must be having an awful time about now, but it wasn't true. Pretty soon he crawls out from under the wigwam. He hadn't been uptown at all. He knew how it would go.

"Well, I sure don't want no more of 'em, Huck."

In three nights, them no-goods took in four hundred and sixty-five dollars. I never seen money come in like that before. After they went to bed that night, Jim asked me, "Don't it surprise you the way those kings carry on, Huck?"

"No," I says. "It don't. It's in their blood."

"Well, I sure don't want no more of 'em, Huck. These two is all I can stand."

"It's the way I feel too, Jim. I wish we could hear of a country that's out of kings."

I went to sleep. Jim didn't call me when it was my turn. He often done that. When I waked up, he was sitting there moaning. I knowed why. He was thinking about his wife and his children. He was homesick. I got to talking to him about his family. What made him sad was hearing someone hit something on the bank. It reminded him of a time when he treated his daughter badly.

"Little 'Lizabeth was only four years old when she got scarlet fever," he said. "But then she got well. So one day I says to her, 'Shut the door.'

She just stood there, smiling. I told her again, and she still didn't do it. I got mighty mad. I told her I'd *make* her mind, and I slapped her hard. Then I went to the other room. When I come back, the door was still open, and the child was crying. Just then the wind come and slam the door. That child never moved! I crept up behind her and made a noise. She still never moved. Oh, Huck, I bust out crying and grab her up in my arms. The poor thing. Lord forgive old Jim, cause he'll never forgive himself as long as he live! She was deaf, Huck, plumb deaf. And to think I treated her that way!"

CHAPTER TWENTY-FOUR

Next day, we kept going till we saw a town on each side of the river. The duke and the king planned to stop at both towns. Jim said he was tired of laying in the wigwam tied up all day. So the duke said he had an idea. He had Jim dress up in one of the costumes—a long gown and a white wig. Then the duke painted his face and hands blue, so Jim looked like a drowned man. The duke made a sign that said *Sick Arab—out of his head.* He nailed the sign up in front of the wigwam. The duke told him to act like a wild beast if anyone came. Then they would leave him alone. Jim was happy enough with the plan.

We had all bought new clothes on our last stop. The king put his on. Then we saw a big steamboat up ahead. He told me to get our boat and head for the steamer. On the way, we passed a young man on shore. He asked for a ride over to the steamboat.

"Get aboard," says the king. The young man said he thought, at first, that the king was Mr. Wilks. If so, he had not quite gotten there in time. The king asked what Mr. Wilks had missed.

"He's missed seeing his brother Peter die," the young man said. He told about the two brothers from England who Peter Wilks had talked about so much. One could not hear or speak. The other was a minister. They were the only family left except for Peter's daughters. Peter had wanted them to come so they could help the girls divide up the money and property.

The king asked about each daughter. He said he was sad about the two brothers not getting there in time. Then he asked for the names of all the neighbors. He also asked about Peter's wealth. By the time we dropped the young man off at the steamboat, the king had worn him out with the questions. But now the king had a plan.

We went back and got the duke. The king told him everything about the Wilks family. The king practiced talking like an Englishman. He asked the duke to act as if he were deaf. That afternoon, the king, the duke, and I got on a steamboat and rode in to town. The king walked up to some men waiting on the dock. He said, "Can any of you tell me where Mr. Peter Wilks lives?"

They said, "I'm sorry, sir. We can only tell you where he did live until yesterday."

The old man seemed shocked. He leaned against the other and cried, "Our poor brother's gone, and we never got to see him." Then he turned around and made some hand signs to the duke. The duke dropped his bags, and then *he* started to cry.

I never seen anything like them two fakes. It was enough to make a body ashamed of the human race.

The men on the dock told the king about his "brother's" last moments. The king and the duke seemed so sad. I never seen anything like them two fakes. It was enough to make a body ashamed of the human race.

CHAPTER TWENTY-FIVE

The news spread fast. When we got to the house, the street was packed. Three girls stood in the doorway. The oldest, Mary Jane, was red-headed and beautiful. Her face lit up when she saw her long-lost uncles. The king hugged Mary Jane. The other girl hugged the duke. Everybody cried. Then the king looked around for the coffin. When he saw it, he and the duke walked over there together. They took one look and started crying. You could've heard them in New Orleans. I never seen two men leak the way they done. Then everybody did the same, and the place was damp with tears.

Well, by and by, the king gets up. He says a little speech, full of tears and **flapdoodle.**[1] He talks

---

[1] **flapdoodle**—slang for silly or syrupy talk.

about their long journey, and he thanks the people for their kindness. He talks about the families his brother named in his letters. They was almost all there, so they came up and shook hands with the king. Then they smiled and shook hands with the duke, who made signs and said "Goo-goo," like a baby that can't talk.

Mary Jane got the letter her father left behind. The king read it aloud. It gave half the money to the girls and half to the brothers. The girls would get the house and the brothers would get the land and businesses. It told where the cash was hidden in the basement. So these two fakes said they would go down and get it. They told me to come along with a candle. When they found the bags, my how the king's eyes did shine. They counted out the money, but it came up short. They didn't want folks to think they took some, so they added some of their own to the pile. Then they came up with an idea.

"Let's go upstairs and give the money to the girls," the duke says. "Then they'll trust us, for sure." The king agreed. They went upstairs, and the king gave another speech. He said they couldn't rob the girls of anything, so he wanted them to have it all. The girls hugged and kissed them. Everyone shook their hands. Then Peter Wilks's doctor came in.

When the people told him this was Harvey Wilks, Peter's brother, he did not believe it. He called the king and the duke fakes. He knew they were not Englishmen by the way the king talked.

The people told the doctor not to hurt Harvey's feelings. It was no use. He turned to the girls and warned them not to be fooled. "I was your father's friend," he says. "I want to protect you from this tramp. Mary Jane Wilks, you know me. Now listen to me. Throw this man out, will you?"

"Here is my answer," Mary Jane said. She lifted the bag of money and put it in the king's hands. "Take all the money and invest it for me and my sisters," she said. Everyone clapped.

"A time will come when you'll feel sick about this day," the doctor says.

"All right, doctor," the king smiles. "When we do, we'll send for you." They all laughed and said he'd made a hit.

CHAPTER TWENTY-SIX

When they was all gone, Mary Jane gave her own room to "Uncle Harvey." She put William, or the duke, in another room. I slept in the attic. That night they had a big supper with their friends. I waited on the king and duke. The girls' servants waited on the rest. When it was all done, me and the other daughter had supper in the kitchen. She got to asking me about England.

"Did you ever see the king?"

"Sure. He goes to our church," I said.

"I thought he lived in London," she said.

"Well, he does."

"But I thought you lived in Sheffield."

I had to choke on a bone to get time to think. "He only goes to our church in the summer time. He come there to take sea baths."

"Sheffield ain't on the sea."

"Well, who said it was?"

"Why, you did."

"I didn't neither."

"You did!"

The talk went downhill from there. After about a half-hour, she says, "Ain't you been telling me a lot of lies?"

"No, none of it. Not a lie in it," says I.

"Well, I'll believe some of it, but I won't believe all of it."

"What is it you won't believe?" says Mary Jane, stepping into the room with her sister Susan behind her. "It ain't right for you to talk to a stranger that way. You should feel ashamed."

I felt bad to think this was the sweet girl that snake was going to rob of her money.

"But he said—"

"It don't matter what he said. You must treat him kindly."

I felt bad to think this was the sweet girl that snake was going to rob of her money. So I says to myself, I'll steal the money back. I'll hide it. Then when I'm away down the river, I'll write a letter and tell Mary Jane where it's hid.

The king's room was dark when I got there, so I thought I would hide and wait for them. I could listen to their talk and find out where they put the money. I hid behind the dresses hung by the wall. The duke and the king soon came in.

"I'm worried about that doctor," says the duke. "I think we'd better get out of here before morning with what we've got."

"What?" the king says. "And not sell the rest of the property?"

The duke said the bag of gold was enough. He didn't want to rob the girls of everything they had.

"Don't worry," says the king. "When the people who buy the property find out about us, they'll give it back. These here orphans won't suffer. Besides, they're young. They can earn a living."

Well, at last the duke gave in. He still said it was foolish to stay, with that doctor hanging over them. But the king said not to worry. The whole town was on their side.

So they got ready to go downstairs again. Then the duke says, "I don't think we put that money in a good place. What if a servant finds it?"

The king pulled the money back from under the curtain, two feet from where I stood. They shoved it under the bed and said it would be safe. But I knowed better. I had it out of there before they was downstairs. I put it in my room till everyone went to bed. Then, in the middle of the night, I took it and went down the ladder.

CHAPTER TWENTY-SEVEN

I tiptoed down the hall and got downstairs. I peeped in through a crack in the dining room door. The coffin was in the parlor. There weren't nobody in there but the remainders of Peter, so I went on through. Just then, I heard somebody coming down the stairs behind me. I ran into the room and took a look around. The only place I could hide the bag was in the coffin. I tucked the bag under the lid.

The person coming was Mary Jane. She went to the coffin and kneeled down. She begun to cry. I slid out of the room and went back to bed, feeling sad. I feared someone would find the money when they screwed down the lid. If not, I would have to write to Mary Jane later and tell her to dig up the grave to get the money.

The next day the undertaker came and set up all the chairs. The people soon began to arrive. They filed around the coffin to look at Peter's face quickly. I worried about whether they saw the money bag. Still, overall, the funeral was very good. Afterward, I saw the undertaker close the coffin and screw it down. They buried Peter, and we come back home. I watched everyone's faces, but they didn't tell me anything.

The king told everyone he had to get back to England, so he would have to hurry and sell all the land he had just been given. He planned to hold a sale two days after the funeral. By then, he had already sold off the servants, splitting up a mother and two sons. The girls cried and hung onto the servants' necks. A good many said it was wrong to split up the mother and the children. The old fool went on in spite of it.

On auction day, the king and duke woke me up at dawn. The king says, "Was you in my room?"

"No, your majesty," I says.

"Have you seen anybody else go in there?"

I thought a while. "Well, I seen the servants go in there. They tiptoed away, so as not to wake you, I thought."

The king and the duke stood there thinking. I asked what was wrong. They said it was none of my business and went down the ladder. Then the king turned back and said I should've told him when I saw someone go in his room.

CHAPTER TWENTY-EIGHT

It was time to get up, so I went down the ladder. As I passed the girls' room, I saw Mary Jane crying. I went in there and says, "Miss Mary Jane, tell me your troubles."

It was the servants. She said she could never be happy in England knowing the mother and children weren't going to see each other no more.

"But they will in two weeks!" says I. She wanted to know why. I had said too much, too soon. But for once, telling the truth looked safer than telling a lie.

"Miss Mary Jane, is there a place you could go for a few days."

"Yes. Mr. Lothrop's. Why?"

"Never mind. If I tell you how I know the servants will come back, will you go to Mr. Lothrop's?"

She agreed, so I told her to brace herself and take the news quietly. Then I said, "These uncles of yours ain't no uncles. They're fakes." It jolted her, of course. Still, I told her the details. She wanted to have them tarred and feathered right away. I told her that another person would be hurt if she did that. If she could just go to Mr. Lothrop's, her face wouldn't let on that she knew just yet. I told her to come back that night and put a candle in the window. If I didn't come back by eleven, she'd know I was gone and safe. Then she could spread the news.

"There's one more thing," I said. "I stole that bag of money to give it to you. I know where I hid it, but I'm afraid it ain't there no more. I'm awfully sorry, Miss Mary Jane. I had to put it in the first place I saw."

"It wasn't your fault. Where did you hide it?"

I couldn't say it, so I wrote it on a piece of paper. It made my eyes water to think about it. Her eyes watered too when I gave her the paper.

"I'll pray for you," she said as she left.

Pray for me! If she knowed me, she'd take an easier job. But I bet she done it, just the same.

Well, they held the sale in the public square that afternoon. It went on and on until almost everything was sold. About that time, a steamboat landed. In about two minutes, up comes a crowd, yelling and laughing.

"Look what we got. Two sets of brothers of old Peter Wilks. Take your pick!"

CHAPTER TWENTY-NINE

The people were walking with a very nice looking old gentleman and a younger one with his arm
in a sling. The duke never let on that he knew what
they were saying. As for the king, he gazed down
sadly at the new brothers. He acted like it made his
heart ache to see such fakes. Lot of people gathered
around him, to show whose side they were on.

Pretty soon the older man who had just come
began to speak. He really *sounded* like an Englishman. He turned to the crowd and says, "This is a
surprise to me. My brother and me had trouble on
the way. He broke his arm, and our bags got put off
in the wrong town. I am Peter Wilks's brother
Harvey, and this is his brother William, who can't
hear nor speak. He can't even make signs much,
now that he's got only one hand to work with. We
are who we say we are. In a day or two, when I get

my bags, we can prove it. Until then, we'll just go to the hotel and wait."

The king laughed and said, "Broke his arm— very likely, ain't it? Lost their bags. That's mighty good." He laughed again, and so did almost everybody else. Three men did not laugh. One was the doctor. Another was the lawyer. The third was a big rough man who stepped up to the king and said, "If you're Harvey Wilks and you came here from Cincinnati the night before the funeral, why were you down the river in a canoe the morning before the funeral?"

"Why, I wasn't."

"It's a lie. I live up there. I saw you go by with Tim Collins and a boy."

The doctor says, "Would you know the boy again if you was to see him?"

"I think I would. Why, there he is now, right over there." It was me he pointed at. The doctor says, "It's our duty to see that no one gets away till we look into this thing."

The doctor led me by the hand, and we all walked to a hotel and went into a big room. First the doctor says, "I don't want to be too hard on these two men, but I think they're fakes. If they aren't, they won't mind us sending for the money and keeping it till they prove they're right."

Everybody agreed to that. But the king looked sad and said, "I wish the money was there, but it ain't."

"Where is it then?"

"Well, when my niece gave it to me to keep for her, I hid it inside my bed. I didn't want to bank it for the few days we'd be here. The house servants stole it the very next morning. My servant here can tell you."

I could see nobody believed him. One man asked me if I saw the servants steal it. I said, "No, but I seen them sneaking out of the room. I thought they was afraid they had waked up my master and was trying to get away."

Then the doctor says, "Are you English too?"

I says yes, and some of them laughed.

Well, then they asked questions for hours. The king spun his yarn[1] and then the old gentleman told his. By and by, the old gentleman said, "Is there anybody here who helped bury my brother?"

"Yes," says somebody. "Me and Ab Turner done it."

Then the old man turns toward the king and says, "Perhaps this gentleman can tell what was tattooed[2] on his chest?"

---

[1] spun his yarn—slang for told his stories.

[2] tattooed—mark made by pricking the skin with a needle and putting ink under it.

The king turned white. Everyone looked at him. Pretty soon he smiled. "I can tell you what's tattooed on his chest. It's just a small, thin, blue arrow. If you don't look close, you can't see it."

The new old gentleman turned to Ab Turner and his partner. His eyes light up. He asks, "Did you see any such marks?"

"We didn't see any," they both said.

"Good," says the old man. "Now, what you did see was his initials—P B W, right?"

"No," they said. "We never seen any marks at all."

Well now everybody started calling both sets of brothers fakes. But the lawyer jumped on the table and yelled, "There's one way to find out. Let's go and dig up the body and look."

They took the four men and me by the collar.

They marched us along to the graveyard, a mile and a half down the river. Everyone carried on like wildcats. I didn't know what they'd do to me if they didn't find them tattoo marks. The husky one dragged me by the hand, and I had to run to keep up.

When they got to the graveyard, they started digging with no light but the flicker of the lightning. They dug and dug like everything. The rain started, and the thunder boomed, but them people didn't stop. At last they got the coffin and broke open the lid. They all crowded around to see.

All of a sudden the lightning let out a stream of light. Somebody called out, "Look! There's the bag of gold!" The man who held me let out a cheer, like everybody else. He let go of me to get in and take a look. I ran for the road in the

When I got to the raft, Jim was coming for me with both arms spread. He was full of joy.

dark as fast as I could. I almost flew back through town toward the house. It looked all dark at first. Then just as I ran by, *flash* comes the light in Mary Jane's window! My heart swelled up. She *was* the best girl I ever did see.

When I got to the raft, Jim was coming for me with both arms spread. He was full of joy. But when I saw him, my heart shot up and I fell off the boat. I had forgot he was painted up like a drowned Arab. It scared the livers and the lights out of me.

In two seconds, away we went, sliding down the river by ourselves. It did seem so good to be free again. But pretty soon, I heard oars in the water. It was the king and the duke, rowing out to the raft. It was all I could do to keep from crying.

CHAPTER THIRTY

When they got aboard, the king shook me
by the collar. He says, "Tryin' to get rid of us,
were you?"

I told him they let me go early, and I thought he
and the duke were already dead by the time I got
to the raft. So the king let go of me and began to
cuss[1] that town and everybody in it. Then the duke
told him it was his own fault, and they get to argu-
ing. Finally, they started to wonder who put the
money in the coffin. Each one thought the other did
it. They argued till the duke went for the king's
throat. So the king finally says, "Enough! I own up!
I did it."

"If you ever deny it again, I'll drown you," says
the duke. "I never seen such an old bird wanting to
gobble up everything. And then you blamed those

---

[1] cuss—to curse or swear.

servants! And now I know why you wanted to add our money to the pile. You wanted to take my cut from the Royal Nonesuch money. Well, now you see what you *got* by it. They've got their money *back*."

The king felt so bad, he went into the wigwam and drank. The duke went in pretty soon, and he started drinking too. In about half an hour, they were thick as thieves[2] again. Of course, when they went to sleep, we had a long talk, and I told Jim everything.

---

[2] thick as thieves—phrase used to mean "great friends."

CHAPTER THIRTY-ONE

We didn't dare stop again for days and days. We went south till we came to a place where moss hangs down on the trees like gray beards. Them two cheats thought they were out of danger, so they begun to work the towns again.

First they gave a talk on drinking, but they didn't make enough money for them both to get drunk on. Then they started a dancing school, but they didn't know how to dance, so the people chased them out of town. They tried doctoring, and telling fortunes, and a little of everything. They couldn't seem to have no luck. At last they came up with a meaner plan than ever.

Early one morning, we hid the raft below a town named Pikesville. The king went ashore. He told us to stay on board till he saw whether the people in the town had heard about the Royal

Nonesuch yet. If he didn't come back by noon, me and the duke would know it was all right to come along.

Jim and I knew something was going on. We thought maybe the king was going to rob a house. If so, we didn't want to have anything to do with it. We wanted to leave first chance we got. Well, he didn't come back by noon, so me and the duke went to town. We looked all over and finally found him with some men crowded around him. The duke started yelling at the king for being such an old fool. I saw my chance, so I took off, ran all the way back, and called out, "Untie the raft, Jim. We're going!"

"He's a runaway slave, and they've got him. There's a two-hundred-dollar reward on him."

But there was no answer. Jim was gone! I ran around in the woods, shouting for him, but it weren't no use. Pretty soon I went out on the road and saw a boy walking. I asked him if he'd seen someone who looked like Jim.

"Yes," he says. "Down to Silas Phelps's place. He's a runaway slave, and they've got him. There's a two-hundred-dollar reward on him."

"Who nailed him?"

"It was an old man—a stranger. He sold his part for forty dollars, because he's got to go up the river and can't wait."

"Maybe there's something wrong, if he'll sell so cheap," I says.

"No, it's true. I seen the handbill myself. It tells all about that slave and the **plantation**[1] he's from, down below New Orleans."

After he left, I went to the raft and sat down to think. I thought till I wore my head out. I couldn't believe it. After all we'd done for them two, they had the heart to sell Jim and make him a slave again all his life. They even had the heart to sell him for forty dirty dollars.

First I thought I should write a note to Miss Watson and tell her where he was. But I soon gave up on that idea. She'd be so mad, she would sell him again. If she didn't, she would treat him badly. And what would people think of me? The more I studied it, the more low-down I felt. In a way, I had stole an old woman's servant. It made me shiver. I almost made up my mind to pray, to see if I could be a better boy. So I kneeled down. But the words wouldn't come. I knowed very well why. It was because my heart weren't right. I was pretending to

---

[1] **plantation**—large farm or estate where cotton, tobacco, or tea is grown.

give up sin, but inside, I was holding on to a big sin. I was trying to make my mouth say I would do the right thing. But deep down, I knowed I wouldn't, and He knowed it. You can't pray a lie.

I thought maybe I could pray if I wrote Miss Watson the letter first, so I sat down and wrote it. I felt good and clean of sin, for the first time in my life. I knowed I could pray now. But first I laid the paper down and got to thinking about Jim. I thought about our trip down the river. I saw him before me, in the day and at night, in moonlight and in storms, talking, singing, and laughing. I couldn't seem to find any hard feelings for him, only good ones. I saw him taking my night watchman shift on the boat, so I could sleep. I saw how glad he was to see me when I came back out of the fog and again in the swamp, up there where the feud was. At such times, he would always call me honey. He would do everything he could think of for me. He said I was his best and only friend. Just then I looked down and seen that paper.

He would do everything he could think of for me. He said I was his best and only friend.

I picked it up and held it in my hand, shaking. I had to decide, forever, between two things, and I knowed it. If I tore up the paper, I'd never get to heaven. If I didn't, Jim would never go free. I held my breath and said, "All right, then. So I never get to heaven." Then I tore it up.

That night I hid out. The next morning I put on my store clothes. I landed the boat near where I thought Phelps's place was. Then I filled up the canoe with water and loaded rocks into it. I sunk her where I could find her again when I wanted to.

Then I went up the road until I saw a sign that said "Phelps's Sawmill." At the same time, I ran into the duke. He was sticking up a bill for the Royal Nonesuch's performance. He looked shocked to see me, but glad.

"Hello!" he says. "Where's the raft? Got her in a good place?"

"I thought you could tell *me* where it is."

"How's that?"

"Well, when I was in town yesterday, a man offered me ten cents to help him bring back his lost sheep. So I went along. When we were dragging the sheep along, it jerked loose and run, and we had to chase it. We never got him till dark. When I got back to the raft, it was gone. I says to myself, 'They left, and they took my servant, which is all I've got in the world. Now I'm in a strange country with no way to make my living.' So I sat down and cried. I slept in the woods all night. So where is the raft? And where is poor Jim?"

"I don't know. That old fool made a trade and got forty dollars. He was gambling it all away when we saw him yesterday. When I got him home last night and found the raft gone, I thought *you* stole it."

> "I says to myself, 'They left, and they took my servant, which is all I've got in the world.'"

"I wouldn't leave Jim. He's the only property I have in the world."

"We never thought of that. Fact is, we'd come to think of him as *our* property, after all the trouble we went to for him. So when we saw the raft gone and our money gone too, we thought we'd have to give the Royal Nonesuch another try."

He asked for some money, and then he asked whether Jim would tell on them.

"How could he tell on you? Ain't he run off?" I says.

"No! That old fool sold him."

"Sold him?" I says, and I begun to cry. "Where is he? I want him back."

"Well you can't get him back. And if you'd ever tell on us—" I never see the duke look so mean. But then he looked sad. He stood there thinking awhile, then he said, "We got to be here three days. If you'll keep quiet and keep Jim quiet, I'll tell you where he is."

So I promised. He started to give the name of Silas Phelps and then stopped. He couldn't trust me. He wanted me out of the way for three days. So he says, "The man that bought him is Abram Foster. He lives forty miles back here in the country."

"All right," I says. "I can walk it in three days."

"Good. Start now, and don't stop and talk to anyone on the way."

I headed out for the back country. I felt like he was watching me, so I went about a mile. Then I stopped and went back through the woods toward Phelps's. I wanted to find Jim and keep him quiet until they left. Then I wanted to be rid of them for good.

When I got to the Phelps's it was all still and hot. The farm hands had gone to the fields. Flies hummed in the air, and the breeze made the leaves quiver like whispering spirits. It felt like everybody was dead and gone.

Phelps's was one of these little one-horse cotton plantations. They all look alike. It had a rail fence with a log **stile**.[1] It had some sickly grass patches in the big yard, but mostly it was smooth and bare. It had a big white log house and a separate kitchen where hound dogs slept by the door. Behind the kitchen sat a smokehouse for smoking meat, and three slaves' cabins on the other side of that. One little hut sat all by itself down against the back fence. You could see some out buildings,[2] a few

---

[1] **stile**—steps alongside a fence, so a person can get over it but a sheep cannot.

[2] out buildings—sheds or barns.

shade trees, and a garden. Beyond that the cotton field began, and then the woods.

I climbed the back stile and headed for the kitchen. I could hear the hum of a spinning wheel,[3] the loneliest sound in the world. When I got halfway there, the dogs got up and ran for me. I stood still. I was kind of a hub in a wheel, with the spokes made of barking dogs. I hoped I would know the right words to say.

A slave woman come running out of the kitchen. She yelled at the dogs and hit them. They all ran off, then came back wagging their tails, ready to make friends with me. There ain't no harm in a hound, nohow.

Three little children hung onto the woman's gown. And here comes the white woman running from the house, about forty-five or fifty years old. Behind her came her children. She was smiling all over.

"It's you, at last! Ain't it?"

I said, "Yes" before I thought.

She hugged me tight. Then she gripped me by both hands and cried. She says, "You don't look as much like your mother as I thought you would, but I'm so glad to see you. Children, it's your cousin Tom. Tell him howdy."

---

[3] spinning wheel—wheel used for stretching cotton or wool into thread.

She said they'd been looking for me for days, and she asked me to call her Aunt Sally. I told her the boat had a breakdown, and that's why we were late.

"Your uncle's been up to town every day when the ferry comes, hoping to bring you home. He went there an hour ago. You must've met him on the road."

"No, I didn't see nobody, Aunt Sally. The boat landed early, so I left my bags there and went to look around out in the country. So I came here the back way."

"Who did you give your bags to?"

"Nobody."

"Why, child, they'll be stolen!"

"Not where I hid them."

I wanted to get the children aside and ask them some questions, to find out who I was. But I didn't get the chance. Mrs. Phelps suddenly says, "You ain't told me a word about Sis, nor any of them. Tell me what they're doing."

Well, I couldn't get out of this one. I thought I may have to risk the truth. I opened my mouth to begin, but she pushed me behind the bed and says,

"Here he comes! Stick your head down. I'll play a joke on him."

Mrs. Phelps ran to the door and yelled, "Has he come?"

"No," says her husband.

"Goodness!" she says, "Where in the world could he be?"

"I don't know," says the old man. "It makes me uneasy."

"Maybe you missed him on the road."

"Why, Sally, I couldn't miss him along the road. You know that."

"Dear, dear, what will Sis say?"

"Oh, don't worry me more. I'm afraid something's happened to the boat."

"Why, Silas. Look up the road. Ain't that somebody coming?"

He sprang to the window. Mrs. Phelps stooped down and gave me a pull. When he turned around, there she stood, smiling, while I stood sweating.

"Why, who's that?"

"Who do you think? It's *Tom Sawyer!*"

I almost fell through the floor. The old man grabbed my hand and shook it. The woman danced around and laughed. Then they both asked questions about Sid, Mary, and the rest of the tribe.

I was so glad to find out who I was. I told them all about the Sawyer family. I told them how it took three days to fix the boat, and that was why I was late. Being Tom Sawyer was easy, until I heard a steamboat coughing along down the river. I says to myself, suppose Tom Sawyer comes down on that boat? What if he walks in here and says my name before I can keep him quiet? I couldn't have it that way. So I told the folks I would go and get my bags. The old man wanted to go with me, but I said I could drive the horse myself.

CHAPTER THIRTY-THREE

When I was halfway to town, I saw a wagon coming. Sure enough, it was Tom Sawyer. "Hold on!" I says. His mouth dropped open.

"I ain't never done you no harm," he said. "So what you want to come back and haunt me for?"

"I ain't come back. I ain't been gone," I says.

"You mean, you weren't ever killed at all?"

"No. I played a trick on them. Feel my arm if you don't believe me."

So he done it, and he knew it was me. He was so glad to see me again, he didn't know what to do. I told him it was a grand adventure. I'd tell all about it later. First we had to come up with a plan.

"I've got it," Tom said. "Take my trunk in your wagon and act like it's yours. I'll come in a half-hour. Don't act like you know me."

"All right. But there's one more thing that nobody knows but me. There's someone here that I'm trying to steal out of slavery, and his name is Jim—old Miss Watson's Jim."

"What!" he says. "Why Jim is—"

"I know what you'll say, but I'm going to steal him anyway."

His eyes lit up, and he says, "I'll *help* you steal him!"

We put the trunk in my wagon. He drove away, and so did I. I was so happy, I forgot to go slow. The old man couldn't believe that horse made such good time. When Aunt Sally saw Tom's wagon coming, she says, "Why, there's a stranger coming. Put on another plate for dinner."

Tom walked right up to the door and lifts his hat before Uncle Silas.

"Mr. Archibald Nichols?"

"No, my boy. Nichols's place is three miles down. But you must come in and eat dinner with us. Then we'll take you down there."

Tom thanked them and came in. He said he was William Thompson and made up stories about

> *"But there's one more thing that nobody knows but me. There's someone here that I'm trying to steal out of slavery, and his name is Jim—old Miss Watson's Jim."*

where he was from. He went on and on. At last, still talking, he reached over and kissed Aunt Sally right on the mouth. She jumped up and wiped it off with the back of her hand.

"You bold boy! What do you mean by kissing me?"

He looked kind of hurt, and says, "I didn't mean nothing, ma'am. I thought you'd like it."

"Why, you born fool!" She picked up a stick and shook it at him. "What made you think I'd like it?"

"They told me you would."

"Who's *they*?"

"Well, just everybody." He looked around the table for a friendly face and stopped on mine. "Tom, didn't you think Aunt Sally would open her arms and say, 'Sid Sawyer!'?"

"My land!" she says, breaking in. "You rascal, to fool me like that."

She went to hug him, but he made her ask him first. So she did. She hugged and kissed him, and then so did the old man. Then when things got quiet, she said, "I never seen such a surprise. We were only looking for Tom. Sis never wrote to me about anybody coming but him."

"It's because I begged and begged. At the last minute, she let me come. Me and Tom thought it would be a good surprise for him to come first and me to drop in as a stranger. But it was a mistake, Aunt Sally. This ain't no healthy place for a stranger."

We all talked over lunch and into the afternoon. No one said anything about the runaway slave. Finally that night, one of the little boys asked, "Can Tom and Sid and me go to the show?"

His father said no, because the runaway slave said it was not fit to watch. So Jim had told on them.

Tom and me was to sleep in the same room. We said we were tired and went to bed. Then we climbed out the window and slid down the lightning rod, a pole that catches the lightning and keeps it away from the house. I thought we'd better go warn the king and duke. By the time we got to town, we saw a crowd of people banging tin pans and and yelling. They had the king and the duke all covered with tar and feathers. I felt sorry for them. People can be awful cruel to one another. I felt to blame, somehow, though I hadn't done nothing.

CHAPTER THIRTY-FOUR

We stopped talking and got to thinking. Pretty soon Tom says, "I bet I know where Jim is—in that hut. Didn't you see a servant go in there with some dinner?"

"I thought that was food for a dog."

"Well, it wasn't, because part of it was watermelon."

"Well, I never thought about a dog not eating watermelon."

"The servant unlocked the **padlock**[1] when he went in and locked it up again when he left. The watermelon shows it's a man in that hut. The lock shows it's a **prisoner.**[2] Now work your mind and let's think of a plan to steal Jim."

---

[1] **padlock**—lock with a U-shaped bar that can open or snap shut.

[2] **prisoner**—person held against his/her will and unable to go free.

I had an idea that we steal the key at night and leave on the raft the next day. Tom said my plan was too easy. It wouldn't create a stir. Pretty soon he came up with a plan that had more style. So that night we went down to look at the hut. We saw a window up high. I said we could help Jim climb out, but Tom said that was too easy.

"Well, then," I says. "We could saw him out, the way I done before I was murdered."

"That's more like it," he says. Between the hut and the fence, on the back side, was a **lean-to**.[3] The door was locked. Tom opened it, and we went in. It had some tools in it. It had no door to the cabin. Tom was joyful. He says, "We'll dig him out through this wall. It'll take a week."

The next morning we went down to make friends with Nat, the man who fed Jim. He was filling a tin pan with bread and meat. He had a nice face, and he tied up his hair with thread to keep witches off. He said the witches had been making noise a lot at night. Tom asked if he was going to feed the dog.

"Yes," he chuckled. "It's a mighty funny dog. You want to look at him?"

---

[3] **lean-to**—rough shed with a sloping roof resting against the side of another building.

"Yes." It wasn't in our plan, but we went right into the dark cabin. Sure enough, there was Jim.

"Why, Huck! And ain't that Mister Tom?" he called.

The servant came in and said, "Do you know these two?"

Tom looked at the servant and said, "Does *who* know us?"

"Why, this here runaway slave. Didn't he just call out your names?"

Tom turns to me and says, "Did you hear anybody call out?"

"I ain't heard nobody say nothing."

Then he says to Jim, "Did you call us?"

"No, sir," says Jim. "*I* ain't said nothing, sir."

Tom turned to the servant and said, "What made you think someone called out?"

"Oh, it's the dad-blamed witches, sir," the poor servant said. "They're always at it. Please don't tell nobody about it, sir."

Tom gave him a dime and said he wouldn't tell nobody. The servant stepped out the door to look at the dime and bite it to see if it was good. Tom turned and whispered to Jim, "Don't say you know us. If you hear digging at night, it's us. We're going to set you free."

Jim only had time to grab us each by the hand and squeeze it. Then the servant came back. We told him we would come and visit again. He said he would like us to come at night, because it's good to have folks around when the witches are out.

CHAPTER THIRTY-FIVE

Before breakfast, we went down into the woods to pick a spot where we could dig a tunnel. Tom said, "Darn it, this whole thing is just too easy. There ain't no watchman to drug. There ain't even a dog to give sleeping pills to. And there's Jim chained by one leg to his bed. Why, all you got to do is lift up the bed and slip off the chain. While I'm thinking of it, we got to hunt up a saw."

"What do we want a saw for?"

"To saw the leg of Jim's bed off."

"But you just said we could lift it up and slip off the chain."

"Whoever heard of getting a prisoner loose in such an easy way? No, in the best books, they saw the bed leg in two and eat the sawdust, so it can't be found. Then, to get away quickly, you kick the leg and slip off the chain."

He put his chin in his hand, thinking. Pretty soon, he shakes his head and says, "No. It wouldn't do. We don't really need to."

"To what?" I says.

"To saw Jim's leg off," he says.

"Good land!" I says. "What would you want to do that for?"

"Some of the best experts has done it. They couldn't get the chain off, so they just cut their hand or leg off. But we don't really need to, and Jim may not like it anyway. So we'll let it go. But he can have a rope ladder. We can tear up our sheets and make him a ladder. We can send it to him in a pie. It's mostly done that way. And I've ate worse pies."

"Why, Tom," I says, "Jim ain't got no use for a rope ladder."

"He has got use of it. He can hide it in his bed, can't he? That's what they all do. Don't you think they'll want clues after he's gone?"

"Well," I says, "if it's in the rules, let him have it. But Tom, if we go tearing up sheets, Aunt Sally's going to get mad."

"Oh, shucks, Huck Finn. We'll just borrow a sheet off the clothesline. And a shirt too, so Jim can use it as a journal."

"But Jim can't write."

"He can make marks on the shirt, can't he?

We'll make him a pen out of an old spoon. He can use his own blood for ink. And when he wants to let the world know where he is, he can write on a tin plate with a fork and throw it out the window."

"But nobody can *read* his plates."

"You don't have to be able to read it."

We heard the breakfast horn blowing, so we went to the kitchen. That morning I took a sheet and a white shirt off of the clothesline. Tom said it was okay to call it stealing because we was doing it for a prisoner. So the next day I stole a watermelon and Tom said that wasn't what he meant. It had to be something we really needed. Well, I could see no reward in helping a prisoner if I had to stop and think about it every time I wanted to hog a watermelon.

"Now, what kind of chance would that give him to be a hero? We want to use knives."

The next morning Tom says we need to find some tools to dig out Jim with. I showed him about all the picks and things in the lean-to. He looks at me sadly and says, "Now, what kind of chance would that give him to be a hero? We want to use knives."

"To dig the **foundation**[1] out from under a cabin?"

"Yes."

"That's foolish, Tom."

"It don't matter how foolish it is. It's the *right* way. I've read all the books about these things. Why it took one prisoner thirty-seven years to dig out. And he ended up in China."

"*Jim* don't know nobody in China."

"Why can't you stick to the point, Huck? We'll just have to *pretend* it took thirty-seven years."

"Now, there's sense in that," I says.

---

[1] **foundation**—concrete or packed clay under a building that helps supports the framework.

CHAPTER THIRTY-SIX

When everybody went to sleep that night, we slid down the lightning rod. We went to the lean-to and got to work. First we cleared everything out of the way. Tom said he was right behind Jim's bed now, and we'd dig under it. So we dug and dug with the knives till almost midnight. We was dog tired. Our hands hurt. Yet you couldn't see that we'd done anything, hardly.

"This ain't no thirty-seven year job," I says. "This is a thirty-eight year job."

Tom sighed and stopped digging. Finally, he said, "It ain't right. It ain't moral. But there's just one way to do this. We got to dig him out with the picks and *pretend* it's knives."

"Now you're *talking!*" I said.

"Give me a knife," he said. I gave him a pick ax from the stack of tools. Then I got a shovel and we made the dirt fly. We dug for another half-hour before bed.

Next day Tom stole a spoon and a candlestick in the house to make pens for Jim. I stole three tin plates. That night we slid down the pole and took one of the candles along. We dug for two-and-a-half-hours and the job was done. Then we crept in under Jim's bed and lit the candle. He was so glad to see us, he almost cried. He called us honey. He wanted us to cut the chain off his leg right away. But Tom said that was against the rules and told him all our plans. So Jim said it was all right.

Tom asked a lot of questions. Jim told him that Uncle Silas comes in every day or two to pray with him, and Aunt Sally comes in to see if he has plenty to eat. Tom said we would put small things in uncle's pockets or tie them to aunt's apron strings. He would have to steal them when they came. He also told Jim to watch for the rope pie. We told him how to keep a journal on the shirt and write with his blood. It made no sense to Jim, but he said he would do as Tom told him.

That night, Tom said it was the best fun he ever had in his life. He wished we could leave Jim in prison and spend our lives getting him out, and then leave the job to our children.

> **Tom said it was the best fun he ever had in his life. He wished we could leave Jim in prison and spend our lives getting him out, and then leave the job to our children.**

In the morning we chopped up the brass candlestick. While I talked to Jim's servant, Nat, Tom put the chunks of metal in Jim's cornbread, to see if it would work. We followed Nat in to watch Jim eat. He almost broke his teeth, but he just said it was rocks getting into his bread. Just then, a couple of dogs come in through the tunnel under Jim's bed. Pretty soon there was eleven of them. We had forgot to lock that lean-to door. Nat yelled, "Witches!" and fell over on the dogs. Tom opened the door and threw out a slab of Jim's meat. The dogs went for it, and he shut the door. Then he asked Nat if he had dreamed something.

"Master Sid, I believe I see almost a million dogs or devils. They was all over me. I wish they'd let me alone."

Tom says, "Well, I tell you what I think. They come here at breakfast time because they're hungry. You got to make 'em a witch pie."

"Master Sid, I ain't ever heard such a thing before."

"Well, then, I'll make it myself. After all, you've been good to us and showed us the runaway slave. But you got to be careful. When we bring the pie, you turn your back. Don't act like you see it. And don't look when Jim takes it. And don't ever *handle* the witch things."

"*Handle* 'em, Master Sid? I wouldn't touch 'em for all the money in the world, I wouldn't."

CHAPTER THIRTY-SEVEN

W e went to the trash pile and found an old tin wash pan. We took it down to the **cellar**[1] and filled it with flour. We also stole some nails and dropped a few into Aunt Sally's apron pocket, which was hanging on a chair. We put another one in Uncle Silas's hat band. Tom dropped the spoon into Uncle Silas's coat pocket.

When Aunt Sally come to breakfast, she looked hot, red, and cross. She poured the coffee and said to Silas, "I've hunted high and low. What has happened to your other shirt? It was on the clothesline yesterday. But now it's gone. "

My heart fell down to my lungs and livers. Tom turned kind of blue around the gills.[2] Uncle Silas

---

[1] **cellar**—basement or underground room where food is kept cool.

[2] blue around the gills—embarrassed, guilty-looking.

says, "I can't understand it. I know I took it off, because—"

"Because you ain't got but one on. It was on the clothesline yesterday. But now it's gone. You'll just have to change to a red flannel one till I can get time to make a new one. It'll be the third I've made in two years. I don't know what you do with them. A body'd think you would learn to take care of them."

"I don't know where it is, Sally. I only see them when they're on me."

"Well, it ain't your fault then, I guess. And the shirt ain't all that's gone. There's a spoon gone. Maybe the cow got the shirt, but the cow never took the spoon."

"Why, what else is gone, Sally?"

"Six candles. The rats could've got the candles. You're always going to stop their holes, but you don't do it, Silas."

"Well, Sally, I'm sorry. I'll do it today."

Just then a maid came in and said a sheet is gone off the clothesline. Another one said a brass candlestick is missing. Aunt Sally yelled at everybody until they got real quiet. At last Uncle Silas fished up that spoon out of his pocket. Aunt Sally's mouth dropped open.

"So you had it all along. Likely as not, you've got the other things in there too. Go along now, all of you. Let me get some peace of mind."

Tom and me went and did Uncle Silas a good deed for saving us. We covered up the rat holes for him. Then we waited around the spoon basket till Aunt Sally came along. Tom counted the spoons as I slid one up my sleeve. Tom says, "Why, Aunt Sally, there's still only nine spoons."

We kept fooling her until she thought she was going crazy.

"I know better," she says. "I counted 'em myself." She counted them again anyway and found nine. Then I slipped back the one I had. She counted them again and found ten. Then Tom took one away when she wasn't looking and had her count them again. She counted again and got mad all over again. We kept fooling her until she thought she was going crazy.

That night we put the sheet back on the line and stole one out of her closet. We kept switching them around till she didn't know how many sheets she had. But we still had to worry about that pie. We cooked it in the woods, using three pans of flour. We got burned all over. It took us all night to tear up the sheet and make a lovely rope. We pretended it took nine months. There was rope enough for forty pies, so we threw most of it away.

Nat didn't look when we put the witch pie in Jim's pan. So as soon as Jim was alone, he busted into the pie and took out the ladder. He hid the ladder inside his bed. Then he scratched some marks on a tin plate and throwed it out the window.

CHAPTER THIRTY-EIGHT

Making the pens wasn't an easy job, but writing on the wall was harder. Tom wanted Jim to make a **coat of arms.**[1] Jim said he didn't have one, but that didn't stop Tom. He thought up a fancy one for Jim. It had a dog stepping on a chain, to stand for slavery. It showed a runaway slave and a lot of other things. It had words underneath that said, "the more **haste,**[2] the less speed." He'd seen it all in a book.

"What does it all mean?" I asked.

"We ain't got time to go over that," he says. He wanted to get on to the writing Jim had to do. He had a list of lines Jim could write, about a broken heart, a lonely heart, and thirty-seven years of

---

[1] **coat of arms**—family emblem with pictures and sometimes words that stand for something important about the family.

[2] **haste**—act of hurrying.

prison life. He couldn't make up his mind which line was best, so he said Jim could write them all on the wall. Then Tom remembered that they don't have log walls in a prison, so he said it would be better if Jim wrote on stone.

Jim said a rock would be harder than a log, but Tom told him we'd help him. It took till almost midnight to move a **grindstone**[3] from the mill. We got it to the tunnel, but Jim had to go outside to write on it. So we raised up his bed, slid the chain off, and wrapped it around his neck. Then we crawled out of the hole. Tom marked the letters with a nail and Jim carved them in the stone. Then we helped him fix his chain back on the bed leg.

Before we went to bed, Tom asked, "You got any spiders in here, Jim?"

"No, thank goodness, Master Tom."

"All right, we'll get you some."

"But bless you, honey, I don't *want* none. I'm afraid of spiders. I'd just as soon have rattlesnakes around."

"That's a good idea. Where could you keep it?"

"Keep what?"

---

[3] **grindstone**—flat rock used for sharpening or grinding things.

"Why, a rattlesnake."

That began a long debate. Tom tried to tell Jim a prisoner has to have spiders and snakes for pets if he wants to gain glory. Jim did not want glory. So Tom said maybe rats would do. Jim tried to make him happy by saying he'd take garter snakes. Tom said he could play music for the rats, to tame them. He said the spiders and snakes would be friendly too, if he played music for them. They would swarm all over him and have a good time.

> **Tom tried to tell Jim a prisoner has to have spiders and snakes for pets if he wants to gain glory.**

"Yes, they will, Master Tom, but what kind of time is Jim having?" says Jim. He went along anyway, just to be a good sport. Then Tom asked that Jim grow a flower and water it with his tears. When Jim said he never cries, Tom had an answer. He would bring an onion and put it in Jim's coffeepot in the morning. The smell of the onion would make his eyes water.

Jim put up quite a fuss about having onions in his coffee and **critters**⁴ in his cabin. Tom scolded him and said he had a chance to make a name for himself. He just didn't know enough to be thankful. So Jim said he was sorry. Finally, me and Tom went off to bed.

---

⁴ **critters**—living creatures; that is, the spiders and snakes.

CHAPTER THIRTY-NINE

In the morning, we went to town and bought a rat trap. We put it over the best rat hole. In about an hour, we had fifteen fat rats. Then we put the trap in a safe place under Aunt Sally's bed. But while we went to look for spiders, the little Phelps boy found the rat cage. He opened the door to see if they would come out, and they did. When we got back, Aunt Sally was standing on the bed, yelling. She spanked us both with a tree branch. We had to go catch more rats, but the second batch was not as good as the first.

We got lots of spiders, bugs, frogs, and caterpillars. We also caught some snakes and put them in a bag in our room. By then it was supper time. When we came back after supper, the bag was empty! There was plenty of snakes around the house for a long time after that. They hung from the rafters and landed in your plate or on your neck. Aunt Sally couldn't stand it. We got a licking every time one of our snakes came her way.

We finally got them all into the cabin. You never did see a cabin as joyful as Jim's when they'd all come out to listen to music. Between the rats, snakes, and spiders, there wasn't room for him in his own bed. They kept it lively, because they never slept all at the same time. They all had a circus on him every night.

Well, by the end of three weeks, everything was ready. We sent Jim the shirt in a pie. Every time a rat bit him, he used his own blood to write on the shirt. We had sawed the bed leg and ate the saw-dust, which gave us stomach aches. The only job left was to write a warning letter. Tom's rules said I had to pretend to be a servant to deliver it. I took one of the servant's dresses that night and put it on. Then I carried a note to the door that said, "Beware. Trouble is on the way."

The next night, Tom drew a skull and cross-bones with blood. We put the picture on the front door. The night after that, we put a picture of a coffin on the back door. I never seen a family so scared. If a door banged, Aunt Sally jumped. If anything fell, she'd do the same. Tom said that meant we'd done everything right.

The next day at dawn, Tom went down to the back door. The servant guarding the house had fallen asleep, so Tom stuck a note in the back of his neck. The note said that a gang of Indians was going to steal the runaway slave at midnight that night. The writer of the note said he thought it was wrong, so he would help stop it. He would watch for the band and "baa" like a sheep when they broke into the cabin. Then the family could come out and lock the thieves inside and trap them.

CHAPTER FORTY

W̲e was feeling good after breakfast. We fished all day and checked on the raft. We got home late and had to go to bed after supper. Everybody was worried and wouldn't tell us why. We sneaked down to the cellar to get some food for later. We took it to our room and went to bed. At eleven-thirty, Tom got ready to go to the cabin with the lunch. "Where's the butter?" he asked.

"I set it out on a piece of bread," I said.

"Well, you left it there then," says Tom. "Slide down to the cellar and get it. I'll go stuff straw into Jim's clothes. We'll leave the straw body in bed when we go. Then I'll be ready to "baa" like a sheep.

So out he went, and down to the cellar I went. The hunk of butter and bread were where I left them. I took them and started up the stairs to the main floor. Then here comes Aunt Sally. I dropped the stuff in my hat and put it on my head just before she saw me. She asked what I was doing in the cellar.

"Nothing," I said. "I ain't been doing a thing, Aunt Sally."

She knew better. She said she didn't believe me. So she sent me into the sitting room until she could find out what I'd been doing.

My, but there was a crowd there! Fifteen farmers sat in the room. They were waiting for the gang of Indians Tom mentioned in his note. Every one of these farmers had a gun. They talked in low voices. I wished Aunt Sally would let me go, so Tom and I could leave with Jim before these farmers came after us.

At last she did come. She began to ask me questions. I could hardly talk, I was so scared. Some of the farmers were ready to go out and hunt down the thieves, since it was only a few minutes till midnight. The others told them to wait for the sheep call. The more antsy[1] they got, the more nervous I got. The more questions Aunty asked, the *hotter* I got. Suddenly, a streak of butter melted and

---

[1] antsy—nervous, jittery.

ran down my hot forehead. Aunt Sally saw it and turned white as a sheet.

"Oh, no!" she says. "He's got the brain fever! His brains are oozing out!"

She snatched off my hat. Out came what's left of the butter. She grabbed me and said she grateful it was no worse. "Why didn't you tell me that's why you went to the cellar?" she asked. "I wouldn't have cared."

She sent me to bed, but instead, I slid down the lightning rod and ran to the cabin. I told Tom we didn't have a minute to lose. Then we heard the men tramping to the door. Some of them came into the cabin to wait while the others hid outside. They couldn't see us in the dark, so we slid under the bed and got through the hole. We waited in the lean-to until the footsteps outside got farther away. Then we crept outside and headed for the fence. Me and Jim climbed over it, but Tom's pants caught on the rail. A piece of fence snapped back and made a noise. Someone called out, "Who's that? Answer, or I'll shoot!"

But we didn't answer. We just ran. Bullets whizzed around us, and the farmers turned the dogs loose. The dogs stopped only to say hello to us. We hid to let them all pass, then we followed

> **I felt glad Jim was finally free. Tom felt glad too, except that he had a bullet in his leg.**

along behind the dogs and farmers. At last, we went through the bushes to where we'd tied up our boat. Then we set out for the island where we kept the raft. I felt glad Jim was finally free. Tom felt glad too, except that he had a bullet in his leg. It hurt and it bled quite a lot. When we saw it, me and Jim tore up one of the duke's shirts to bandage it. Tom wanted us to set the raft loose and go, but Jim said he wouldn't leave without getting Tom a doctor first. I told them I'd get in the boat and go find one.

CHAPTER FORTY-ONE

The doctor was a nice old man. I got him up and told him me and my brother had a hunting accident. I said we camped on a raft, and he kicked his gun in his sleep, and it shot him in the leg. The doctor said he would come and help, but he didn't think my boat looked safe enough for two. He took off in my canoe and told me to wait till he got back. While I waited, I tried to get some sleep. When I woke up, it was morning! I went back to the doctor's house, and they said he never came back that night. I thought that meant Tom was in bad shape, so I'd better get back to the island. I hurried off, turned a corner, and ran right into Uncle Silas!

"Why, Tom! Where you been all this time?"

"Just hunting for the runaway slave—me and Sid."

"Where did you go? Your aunt's been worried."

"We was all right. We followed the men and dogs, but they outran us. We lost them. So we took the boat down the river to catch up. Then we got tired and went to sleep. We just woke up an hour ago, and we came to hear the news. Sid went to the post office."

So then Uncle Silas went with me to the post office to get Sid. He picked up a letter while we waited for Sid but, of course, Sid never came. Uncle Silas said we should go home and let Aunt Sally know I was all right. When we got home, she was so glad to see me, she laughed and cried at the same time. She spanked me, but she also hugged me.

The farmers and their wives had all come for lunch. They stood around talking about how crazy that runaway slave was. They saw the things he wrote on the stone and on the bloody shirt. They looked at the rag ladder, the hole under the bed, the sawed-off bed leg, and the straw dummy in the bed. They said he must have had help from a house full of slaves. Aunt Sally told how they stole all those things right out from under their noses. And after all that, the runaway had escaped from the Indians as well as the farmers.

"It must've been spirits," she said, "because our dogs couldn't even track 'em."

She talked about how scared she'd been—so scared that she went upstairs to lock the boys in their bedroom, so they'd be safe. She looked at me funny, and I knew I'd have to tell her why we weren't in the locked room that morning. I thought about it all day. When everyone left, I came and told her that me and Sid heard all the shooting and woke up. We wanted to see what happened, so we slid down the lightning pole. Then I told her what I told Uncle Silas before. She said it was all right. But then she started wondering where Sid was. I offered to go get him, but Uncle Silas wouldn't let me. He said he'd go instead.

At ten o'clock, Uncle Silas came home. He said he hadn't found Sid's tracks. Aunt Sally wanted to wait up for him. First she tucked me in. She mothered me so good, I couldn't look her in the eye. Then she started talking about Sid, saying maybe he was lost, or hurt, or drowned. She cried, and I told her Sid was all right. I thought he would be home in the morning. She told me to keep saying it. When she left, she made me promise to be good and stay inside, for her sake.

I wanted to go see about Tom, but after that, I wouldn't go, not for the world. But I still couldn't sleep. Twice in the night, I slid down the pole and went around front. I saw her sitting there by her candle, crying and looking down the road. I wished I could do something for her. I swore I wouldn't hurt her no more. When I finally came down in the morning, she was asleep at the window.

CHAPTER FORTY-TWO

The old man went uptown before breakfast. He still couldn't find Tom. He and Aunt Sally both sat there looking sad and not eating. Pretty soon, he says, "Did I give you the letter?"

"What letter?"

"The one I got yesterday at the post office."

"No, you didn't give me no letter."

So he goes to get it. She says, "Why, it's from St. Petersburg. It's from Sis."

She was about to open it when she looked up and dropped the letter. She saw Tom Sawyer and that old doctor out the window. Jim was there too, wearing her calico dress, with his hands tied behind him. A lot of people came along, and they had Tom on a mattress.

She ran to Tom, thinking he was dead. Tom turned his head and said something crazy. She said, "He's alive, thank God!" Then she ran into the house to get the bed ready. The old doctor and Uncle Silas helped get Tom into the house. I followed the men to see what they were going to do with Jim.

Some of the men wanted to hang him. Others said it wasn't their right. The owner might show up and make them pay for him. The farmers hit Jim and yelled at him, but Jim never said nothing. Then they took him to his cabin and put his own clothes on him. They chained him up good this time, so he couldn't get away. Just then the doctor came out to take a look.

"He gave up his freedom to help Tom! He ain't no bad slave, gentlemen," the doctor said.

"Don't be so mean to him," he said. "He ain't a bad person. When I found the boy, I couldn't get the bullet out by myself. Tom was out of his mind and wouldn't let me come near. I said I would just have to go get help, even though I didn't want to leave him. Then suddenly, this man comes out of nowhere and says he'll help. He done it, and he done it very well. I knew he was the runaway, so I couldn't leave, or he'd escape again. So we all stayed till this morning. I never saw a better nurse than him. He gave up his freedom to help Tom! He ain't no bad slave, gentlemen," the doctor said.

I was mighty thankful to him for saying it. I knew Jim had a good heart and was a good man. They all agreed not to cuss him out any more, but they locked him up anyway.

By the next morning, Tom was a bit better, so I went in to see him. Aunt Sally said he might wake up in his right mind. Finally, he did. He opened his eyes and said, "Why, I'm at home! Where's the raft? And Jim?"

"It's all right," I said.

"Good! Now that we're safe, did you tell Aunty?"

I was going to say yes, but she said, "About what, Sid?"

"Why, about the way we did the whole thing — how me and Tom set the runaway slave free."

"Good land! This child is out of his mind again!"

"No, I ain't. We did set him free. And we done it proper, too."

He told her the whole story. He said it took weeks and weeks and hours and hours. He told her how we stole everything while she slept. He explained how we sent spoons in her pockets and put rats and snakes in the cabin. He even told her about the escape. Well, when he finally finished the story, she was ready to whip us both. She told us never to mess with Jim again.

Tom looked at me and said, "Hasn't he got away?"

"He sure hasn't," said Aunt Sally. "He's in the cabin again, loaded down with chains."

Tom sat up in bed and said, "Turn him loose! He ain't no slave. He's free!"

"She was ashamed she ever said she'd sell him down the river, so she set him free in her will."

"What does the child mean?" asked Aunt Sally. So Tom told her what he meant.

"Old Miss Watson died two months ago. She was ashamed she ever said she'd sell him down the river, so she set him free in her will."

"Then why on earth did *you* set him free, if he was *already* free?"

"Why, just for the adventure of it!" Tom said. Then he saw someone coming. "Aunt Polly!" he shouted. Aunt Sally turned and ran for her sister and almost hugged her head off. I hid under the bed. She was looking at Tom.

"You'd better turn away. I would if I was you, Tom."

"Oh, dear," said Aunt Sally. "That's not Tom. It's Sid. Why, where is Tom?"

"You mean where's Huck Finn. That's what you mean! Come out from under that bed, Huck Finn."

So I done it. But not feeling bold.

Aunt Sally looked mixed up. So did Uncle Silas when he came in. So Tom's Aunt Polly told all about who I was. She also said Tom was right about old Miss Watson setting Jim free in her will. Aunt Polly had come and see what Tom was up to, since she never got any answers to her letters. They asked what letters.

"Why, I wrote you twice, to ask you what you meant when you said Sid was here."

"Well, I never got the letters, Sis," said Aunt Sally.

Aunt Polly turned to Tom and scolded him. He admitted hiding the letters. She had written a third one to say she was coming.

"I've got that one," said Aunt Sally. "It just came yesterday." I knew she didn't have it, because I did, but I never said nothing.

CHAPTER THE LAST

We had Jim out of the chains in no time. When Aunt Polly and Uncle Silas and Aunty Sally found out how he helped the doctor care for Tom, they made a big fuss over him. Then Tom gave Jim forty dollars for being a good prisoner. Jim said, "There now, Huck. I told you I'd be rich again one day."

Tom said we three should go out and get Indian gear. Then we could have some adventures with the Indians for a while. I said I didn't have the money for it. I thought my father had gone back and taken all the money from Judge Thatcher. If so, he had probably drunk it all up.

"No, he ain't," says Tom.

"And he ain't coming back no more," Jim says, kind of solemn.

"Why, Jim?"

At first he wouldn't tell. Then he reminded me of that houseboat we found with all the clothes and things and the dead man inside. "The dead man was your Pap," Jim said. He hadn't wanted me to feel bad, so he never told me.

Tom is almost well now, and there's nothing left to write about. I'm glad, because if I'd known how much trouble it was to make a book, I wouldn't have done it. And I ain't going to no more. But I got to go to the Indian Territory ahead of the others now. If I don't leave soon, Aunt Sally will adopt me and try to teach me manners. I can't stand the idea of it. I've been there before.

THE END.

YOURS TRULY,
HUCK FINN.